Read, Discuss, and Learn

Using Literacy Groups to Student Advantage

Lisa A. Fisher

ROWMAN & LITTLEFIELD EDUCATION
A division of
ROWMAN & LITTLEFIELD PUBLISHERS, INC.
Lanham • *New York* • *Toronto* • *Plymouth, UK*

This book was placed by the Educational Design Services LLC literary agency.

Published by Rowman & Littlefield Education
A division of Rowman & Littlefield Publishers, Inc.
A wholly owned subsidary of
The Rowman & Littlefield Publishing Group, Inc.
4501 Forbes Boulevard, Suite 200, Lanham, Maryland 20706
http://www.rowmaneducation.com

Estover Road, Plymouth PL6 7PY, United Kingdom

British Library Cataloguing in Publication Information Available

Library of Congress Cataloging-in-Publication Data

Fisher, Lisa A., 1980–
 Read, discuss, and learn using literacy groups to student advantage / Lisa A. Fisher.
  p. cm.
 Includes bibliographical references.
 ISBN 978-1-60709-428-9 (cloth : alk. paper) — ISBN 978-1-60709-429-6 (pbk. : alk. paper) — ISBN 978-1-60709-430-2 (electronic)
  1. Content area reading. 2. Group reading. 3. Student-centered learning. 4. Individualized instruction. I. Title.
 LB1050.455.F57 2010
 372.41'62—dc22   2010010115

♾™ The paper used in this publication meets the minimum requirements of American National Standard for Information Sciences—Permanence of Paper for Printed Library Materials, ANSI/NISO Z39.48-1992.

Printed in the United States of America.

Dedicated to

all students who desire choice in school

and

all those teachers who like a challenge.

Contents

Figures

Tables

Foreword

"Mrs. Fisher, Mrs. Fisher! I just finished my book. Is there a sequel? I hope there is because I want to read more!"

How often do we hear this in the halls of our school? If your school is like most of the schools I have taught in over the past thirty years, it is rare.

The goal for so many of us in education is not just to teach the strategy (or lesson) but also to inspire a love of reading in order to learn and think critically about the material presented. Too often, our reading instruction focuses on discrete skills or concepts but does not include the motivation to read and truly internalize new information.

I listened to Hazel Haley, teacher extraordinaire for over sixty-nine years, speak about the teaching profession in a way that defines using lit groups for student advantage: our job is not just to bring the horse to the water, but also to make the horse thirsty (1999).

One of the qualities of a good reader is that he or she reads. The more a person reads, the better the person will get at it (Gallagher, 2004; Harvey and Goudvis, 2000). Therefore, inspiring a love of reading and at the same time teaching necessary strategies, skills, and concepts will surely be successful.

Mrs. Lisa Fisher did just this through the literacy groups that she researched within secondary-school classes. She acknowledges the adolescent trait of a strong desire to interact socially and combines that with a very tight lesson structure, assigning each individual a specific job in the literacy groups.

The combination of social interaction, role responsibility, and fascinating text choices creates an environment that inspires reading to learn. Beyond the reading, students learn teamwork, interaction skills, critical thinking, comprehension strategies, and, best of all, the desire to read more. Of course, this success does not come easily.

The book you are about to read details possible struggles, setbacks, and obstacles that one may encounter and conquer through the use of literacy groups.

To appreciate the value of this book is also to appreciate my friend and colleague, Lisa Fisher. Lisa is first and foremost a professional educator who continues to grow and learn every day. She came from a childhood that did not include reading. Lisa, in fact, hated to read until she found the first book she truly enjoyed. That did not happen until the end of her high-school experience.

As a result, she struggled to achieve through most of her formative years. Once she found the joy of reading, she never looked back. She dove ahead into all genres of adolescent literature. Then she earned a degree in education and found the research on reading fascinating. She taught herself and became an expert on researchers who have made their mark in education: Richard Allington, Marie Clay, and Janet Allen, to name a few.

Lisa earned her master's degree in reading and further expanded her understanding of all the skills that are necessary in order for someone to be an excellent reader. But she never forgot the biggest thing a good teacher must do: inspire a desire to read across all genres. Because without reading, one cannot learn!

You are to be commended for pursuing your professional development by reading this excellent professional text, a guidebook to the use of literacy groups. As you read this book, envision your classroom as a place that inspires a love of reading to learn in an environment that promotes adolescent inquiry; imagine yourself as the facilitator of this rewarding ambience.

Cynthia Tehan
National Board Certified Teacher of Language Arts,
French, and Drama in Pasco County, Florida

Preface

Reading is like art, abstract and subjective. Each reader derives a different meaning from the text based on several variables, such as experience or background knowledge, feelings or emotional state of mind, and personal understanding or interpretation of the text. I love reading because of these variables and the never-ending challenges that arise; it is not just black or white!

For that reason, my ultimate desire is to inspire every student to find a type of text (e.g., books, magazines) that he or she wants to read and inspire all teachers to embrace the idea of being teachers of literacy within their content areas at the secondary level. Teachers can no longer assume students understand the text simply because they can decode the words on a page.

As a result, this professional text is an inspirational tool and a professional-learning opportunity for current and future secondary teachers, administrators, and curriculum directors to use the idea of literacy groups within their classrooms.

The text is written as a support system and a guide, so that educators will not feel apprehensive about trying something new and making mistakes, and will instead involve students in the learning process at a deeper level.

Fortunately, much ground has been covered pertaining to the idea of literacy groups over the past few years alone, so teachers can feel reassured to know that the research supports the use of literacy groups through several avenues of approach and implementation. In other words, the literacy-group strategy lends itself to individual needs and personalization for each classroom and all content areas (history, math, science, and language arts).

Opportunely, this book is a series of stepping-stones that will lead teachers to a place where literacy is viewed as a positive learning experience by both students and teachers. The goal of this book is that it will be a practical resource guide, providing a progression within the text that will prove to be beneficial in walking teachers through the use of literacy groups within their classrooms.

Thus, this process is told through a typical 365-day journey of secondary students within the public school system. I know teachers will find it to be helpful and applicable to their situations, as well as being enjoyable to read as a professional-learning opportunity.

This book will inspire middle- and high-school teachers, as well as administrators and trainers, to use student-centered learning in the form of literacy groups as a way of increasing student achievement, particularly in the content areas of social studies and science.

Since I am a literacy leader, the experiences shared throughout are explained from the vantage point of my professional research on the topic, and all steps and procedures are given in a form in which they can be adapted for any and all contexts (which is explained in detail throughout the chapters).

The book progresses in the order of occurrence, walking teachers through the process of thinking about literacy groups, creating literacy groups, and, finally, designing the best assessment tools to adequately evaluate students' comprehension or mastery of new content. This makes the book a wonderful tool for training educators to think about and use student-centered learning.

I will share with teachers the possible mishaps and successes in order to assist them to steer clear of the same mistakes, as well as to experience more successes with the use of literacy groups the first time around.

Furthermore, a big picture is painted, from the start, for teachers to visualize as they are guided through the process of using literacy groups. In addition, appendixes A–I offer several examples of students' literacy roles, modeling literacy strategies to roles through guided whole-class instruction and practice, as well as providing reproducible forms for teachers to use and adapt to their needs.

All of this makes this professional text an excellent training tool for administrators and teachers alike; it helps them understand the benefits of student-centered learning, as well as how to make literacy work in all subjects.

Through this process, teachers can get a full representation of each aspect being discussed throughout the book and walk away with a greater understanding and a few valuable classroom resources beyond the content-area textbook to get them started.

It is within the process of literacy groups that I truly believe students enjoy becoming proficient readers and move from learning to read to reading to learn in any content area!

Acknowledgments

I wear many hats in my personal and professional life, as I am sure you do too. I am a woman, a wife, a mommy to four Chihuahuas, a friend, a sister, and a daughter. Most importantly, I am a teacher and lifelong learner! Writing this book has encouraged me to wear my many hats as well; and because of this educational experience, I have learned to be a better teacher, listener, and learner for all students!

Reading, writing, and researching are my passion, and finishing this book is the fulfillment of a dream. I could not have accomplished this dream without the support of my husband, Ryan, who has continuously given up his time with me so I could lock myself in the office for hours a day for three years, and who has always muted the television when I needed an ear to listen for improvements as I read each sentence out loud multiple times.

I read him each chapter so many times he could probably recite the book in his sleep! He was my source of encouragement for writing this professional book, which I would never have done if he had not suggested it after hearing about my teaching experiences year after year and day after day. Thank you, Ryan, for all the suggestions you gave me throughout the years. You are an amazing person, teacher, and husband!

I truly am blessed to have such wonderful friends, who also supported me through the entire process by providing encouragement, suggestions, ideas, and laughter when frustration set in. I also want to say thank you to my friend Maria for meeting me frequently for Sunday lunch so that I could talk about my progress and my frustrations, and bounce ideas off of her.

I have much appreciation and gratitude for my friend and colleague Cindy, who helped edit and revise this book, as well as writing the foreword for it. I truly respect her, and she is more than just a friend and colleague: she is an amazing teacher who is so knowledgeable and compassionate that it shines in the eyes of every student who passes through her doorway.

Thank you, Cindy, for always being there to give me advice and guidance with my instruction, communication, and student interaction. I have grown so much because of your words of love and wisdom.

My biggest thank-you goes out to the students whose voices you can hear throughout the book. They were so patient with me through the videotaping, audio recording, surveying, and interviewing. There is no way this book would even exist without their hard work and dedication to the research (practice and theory) on the use of literacy groups.

Of course, I could not have written this book without the abundance of resources available on the Internet and in other well-respected professionals' written work. It is reading those many, many professional texts that inspired me to always want to improve, so that my students can always get the best out of me! Thank you from the bottom of my heart for the sharing and collaborating that occur among members of our profession.

In view of all this, I am honored that one of many hats I get to wear is a hat that belongs to a teacher. I am grateful for all the lives I have had the privilege of being a part of throughout the years. I hope those students have learned as much from me as I have learned from them. Thank you for allowing the research experience shared within this professional text to add to the many hats you wear in your personal and professional life!

Prologue

We live in an ever-changing society. This is particularly true for our students. This world is not the same as it was ten years ago, much less twenty years ago when many of us were in elementary school. Thus, as teachers, we need to keep up with the change and adapt our teaching style to meet the needs of our diverse American culture.

However, adaptation is not about watering down the content or using easier materials because we think the students cannot master the skills. It is about seeing students' individuality and meeting them halfway to help them become lifelong learners.

As teachers, we should learn to construct our curriculum to inspire students, in order to expand their repertoire of cultures, ethnicities, and diversity. Consequently, teachers who maintain high expectations for their students and hold themselves accountable for their students' successes and willingness are more likely to have students who will reach their highest potential.

Therefore, we should not feel the need for our curriculum to be diminished, but we must believe students can achieve more through innovative approaches that challenge them to think critically. This will lead students to become independent and flexible lifelong learners.

Through this statement of belief, we choose to change literacy instruction through the way we teach strategies, ideas, and skills pertaining to our subject areas. You have decided to explore the succeeding chapters from beginning to end, to guide you through self-reflection and change in the way you teach your curriculum.

Unfortunately, not every teacher wants to learn and grow; but some teachers—like you—are seeking professional growth. You will discover all this book has to offer you in the chapters to come, and this will guide you in enhancing your content, material, and teaching method. The fact that you are reading this book demonstrates that you want the best for your students!

This enhancement is represented in the form of a student-centered classroom. The term comes from the commonly used term *literature circles*, which has been used by teachers of reading and language arts for some time now. Literacy groups are referred to by many titles, such as *literature circles, discussions, studies,* or *book clubs.*

Literacy groups are a form of cooperative learning whereby a group of three to five students get together to dig deeper into a text. This method allows diverse learners to get together to learn about multiculturally rich text pertaining to individual content areas.

In order for teachers to overhaul their subject areas and include innovative teaching methods, they must have arrangement and cooperative learning, so students can master new strategies and skills. It is through this multiple-brain conversation that students develop into independent and flexible learners.

Therefore, each chapter within this professional book will steer you through all the different details pertaining to the use of literacy groups as that newfound instructional approach in your classroom.

However you wish to refer to this new instructional approach is up to you, but research has proved that with such a diverse population in a continuously changing culture, using literature circles (adapted for this text as literacy groups) is an exciting way to learn and to be exposed to multicultural text.

In addition to using literacy groups to promote group discussion and learning through the exploration of text, it is a wonderful modification for English-language learners and struggling readers (Gilmore and Day, 2006). Furthermore, you will learn from the description in each chapter a surefire way to employ literacy groups in your classroom.

In the first chapter, you will get a glimpse into the discussion aspect of literacy groups. Keep in mind that this level of discussion takes months to produce, and the students need to dedicate a lot of hard work and time. So be patient, and it will pay off!

Remember the first time you learned how to do something, such as drive or cook? Most likely, you were not proficient at it overnight!

Reading to learn content material at the secondary level is not about perfection, it is about persistence, and it is important students know and understand this idea. Understanding this idea will allow flexibility so that you and your students can make mistakes and adjust to create the best learning atmosphere possible.

Chapter 2 will provide you with some background knowledge about literacy groups. Several professionals define the term, and a short historical overview is also included, as this teaching method is not a new idea, but is perhaps new to you and your students!

The next chapter guides you through how to establish a student-centered classroom by properly grouping students, as well as appropriately matching students with meaningful content text.

This is where you as a science, social-studies, or language-arts/English teacher will learn how to break down a chapter to use it for group learning, locate grade-level-appropriate text outside the textbook, and utilize the Internet—all for group learning. This chapter will also describe how to match text with themes or topics, and the best way to share the information among your students.

Chapters 4 and 5 break up the different parts of literacy groups and provide several examples to assist you with understanding the process.

Chapter 4 walks you through how to introduce the idea to your class, and how to scaffold each step of the process for your students. Once you finish this chapter, you will have a greater understanding of how to promote independence and flexibility in each of your students.

Chapter 5 provides multiple assessments that are hands-on and creative. In addition, several black-line masters are provided in the appendixes for you to utilize as you deem necessary. The chapters walk you through establishing, maintaining, and assessing literacy groups within the classroom from many different perspectives and on many different levels. This type of approach makes differentiating instruction that much easier.

Keep in mind this is one approach to using literacy groups, and it should be modified for your students' needs. Also, the types of adaptation you do with a group of students will most likely differ from year to year, depending on your students.

The final chapter addresses content adaptations and additional perspectives for the use of literacy groups. There are several respected authors who have books published on the topic (literature circles), each from a different approach and perspective, just as you too will develop a personalized approach and comfort level with the use of group learning once you finish this professional learning opportunity.

Ultimately, at the heart of this book is a desire to help you see how your students can successfully step out of their comfort zone and try something student-centered in the classroom, by taking a journey through the use of literacy groups at the secondary-school level—so that you can be a teacher of differentiated instruction, with all its trials and triumphs.

Enjoy your journey as you read about how you and your students will be inspired to learn in a meaningful way how to become proficient readers for learning secondary content—through flexibility, and with respect for multicultural text and backgrounds within the literacy-group experience!

Make a note to the effect that the best way to approach this book is to do what it discusses with your class, as the book guides you through the process of literacy groups.

If you are a trainer using this text as professional learning, the best way for you to approach this book is through modeling, allowing the participants to practice, and providing follow-up throughout the school year.

Introduction

Students' Voices Create Model Literacy Groups

"I think literacy roles and groups are a great way to improve your reading and vocabulary skills. It is also fun to read exciting books," Timothy shares as he enters the classroom.

Imagine a typical secondary classroom. It is fourth period, right after lunch, in early spring (April), as students pass through the doorway into the classroom. You stand at the door to greet them as they enter.

After you get the class started and warmed up, students participate in a lesson on critical comprehension (determining the author's purpose and tone of text) or take turns recalling major points from your class discussion about plants and animals (science class) the day before, and then you transition into small groups where learning continues to evolve into deeper levels of understanding.

You will notice an increased level of decibels spilling out of the classroom as students engage in small groups. If someone were to just walk in, he or she might think learning was not taking place, but that could not be further from the truth.

Students' conversations overflow with eagerness as they share, discuss, and collaborate within small groups, so do not be afraid of a little controlled and organized chaos. "Hey, I didn't get that when I read last night," one student shouts from across the classroom as another student shares his opinion of the reading from the night before.

These small groups are actually literacy groups in full swing—an extension of the required textbook! Remember that you are dealing with adolescents, so you should kick off literacy groups with a set of objectives in order to guide the students' group discussion and ensure the most on-task learning time.

Also, find a way to pull the class back together; for example, clap your hands and whisper to gain the class's attention and begin your explanation of the agenda for that day.

Another option is to keep a timer on the board or overhead, the kind that beeps. Be specific with your goals and directions, so that distractions (off-task behavior) do not prevent students from reaching a level of higher-order thinking and getting the most out of the literacy-group experience within your class time!

STUDENT INTERACTION

Read the classroom scenario provided in order to gain an understanding of the desired outcome as you continue to explore further into the idea of literacy groups. You will need to keep this scenario in mind as you move from chapter to chapter and develop an awareness of and comfort level with the use of literacy groups within your personal classroom.

Now, take a trip to a classroom that has been using literacy groups from September to April. It is early April in this language-arts class in Tampa, Florida. Imagine, if you will, what all this talk about literacy groups looks like and sounds like.

Students' conversations are quoted as they were stated, and so the syntax, semantics, and sometimes even the clarity represent an early-secondary developmental level. Consequently, this will make some dialogue seem confusing at times, but just keep in mind that the conversation occurs among eleven- and twelve-year-old students and is meant to depict an actual classroom setting with real students.

The purpose of this dialogue is to help you see the end result, so you have a better understanding of the process that will take you to a productive outcome, in which students get the most out of your class and content.

> Class, this is our second week with these books, so you should be approaching the end. Therefore, your goals for today are to first discuss and share your literacy roles in order to bring new meaning to the text. Then share *"what if"* situations in order to challenge your original thinking of the text, [and] determine what the author's purpose and tone are for the reading you did last night and how it is connected to the theme.
>
> Finally, practice oral fluency and read together out loud, being sure to stop and discuss points from the reading. Are there any comments, questions, or concerns before we get started?

The students shake their heads no simultaneously and shuffle around, so the teacher writes the stop time on the white board and begins to circulate in the classroom, to check that students fulfilled their roles from the night before.

Then the teacher chooses a group to work with for about fifteen to twenty minutes, in order to challenge their minds and guide their interaction, as well as reinforcing skills or ideas that they've learned during whole-class instruction.

The teacher stops at one group, sitting at table 5. They are all leaning inward, toward the center of the group. "Okay, let's start. First, we have to share our roles," Christy states as literacy groups get rolling. You want to help your students get to this independent stage, but this will take time and consistency on your part as the facilitator.

"I'll go first, okay?" Caroline suggests, as the discussion director of the group. As the discussion director, Caroline asks questions that require beyond-the-text thinking, monitors the time, and keeps the group focused.

Do not assume students innately know how to do this; you will need to show them how by following an "I do," "we do," "they do," "you do" scaffolding process. (This is explained further in chapters 3 and 4.) "Okay, um, this is from last night. If you had a choice, would you rather stay with your grandfather or risk going to the orphan house, and why?"

Christy quickly shares her opinion, "Grandfather! At least that way I know who I'm with."

"But, um, well, either: I would go to the orphan house because you couldn't find food easily or—" Caroline begins to explain.

"You'd get taken care of by either," Justin quickly interjects.

"Yeah, I guess so," Caroline agrees. "Who do you think broke into the coffee house and why?"

"I don't know because it didn't really give any clues," Christy honestly admits. "It could have been some crazy person or something since there is that disease going around."

"Yeah, like a mugger who was in desperate need," Justin suggests.

"What would you have done if the robbers were in your house?" Caroline questions the group for open-ended responses.

For a minute, all the group members try to respond to the question all at once, out of excitement. Then finally, Justin dominates. "I would have picked up the heaviest object in my house and threw it at him and ran like the wind!"

"I would have actually went into the kitchen, grabbed a knife, and just start throwing knives at the guy, and then I would call the police on my cell phone as I ran!" Christy excitedly shares next.

The discussion that occurs at this time, as compared against those at the start of the school year, needs to demonstrate growth. You and your students will feel proud of the improvement they have demonstrated from month to month. It takes a lot of effort and self-reflection on the part of the students, and on your own part, to get to this point; but as you listen to their conversations, it is worth every bit.

To help your students arrive at higher-level thinking and conversation, you will want to videotape the groups in action. This will allow your students to watch the video and make constructive changes to better their interactions.

Literacy groups will give you the key to success in your classroom. Students will enhance their ability to be readers, better learning your subject because they will be truly invested as individual learners. Continue to see how this group interaction unfolds within this sample dialogue.

"Do you think Matilda will go to the orphan house, and why?" Caroline asks. The group all agrees she will not go to the orphan house because she has her own agenda. This then leaves Caroline to ask her final question, "Why do you think that lady kept hitting Matilda—that lady with the cane?"

"Maybe she was just old," Luke says.

"Maybe she didn't have the sense not to do it," Justin suggests.

"Maybe she's just crazy," Christy nervously adds.

"There are a lot of crazy people in this book, and who's to say Matilda won't end up like the rest of them?" Justin adds at the end of the discussion director's turn. "Her mom did speak harshly to her."

"Her mom isn't mean out of hatred, but out of concern for Mattie to grow up to be the best, like our parents get on to us for similar reasons," Caroline passionately states.

You are still just observing at this point, as the facilitator in your classroom. There is no reason to jump in unless the conversation is weak or lacks depth (higher-order thinking) or students are off task. "It seem like the yellow fever is causing panic just like the Holocaust did in the last book we read, right?" Christy questions.

"Yeah, I was thinking it might have something to do with the theme of understanding loss and death—because remember when that other group shared what they were reading in their group the other day about the boy who died on his bike?" Justin suggests.

"Yeah, that's true. Now, I'm going to share my role," the artful artist states.

The artful artist's job is to illustrate the most important information from the scheduled reading the night before. The artful artist displays each picture to the group members and has them guess what the illustration represents, based on the assigned reading.

"What do you think this is a picture of?" Christy polls the group. The illustration that Christy has drawn and now shares with the group is of a woman lying in a bed and a young girl with tears dropping from her eyes standing at the foot of the bed. The group members then begin stating their interpretations of the illustration. The more you require of your students and the more you hold them accountable, the more effort they will put into the class work and the more the students will get out of the learning experience.

"Matilda's mom," Justin answers.

"Yeah, Matilda's mom in the bed," Christy clarifies.

This part always elicits a lot of conversation among the group members, so you should be concerned if the conversation ends with such simplicity, and you should feel the need to interject—because your students did not demonstrate the higher-level thinking to support their responses as they explained why that illustration was important to the understanding of the text (just as the sample dialogue displays).

"What was the author's purpose [in describing] Mattie's mom in bed, and how is this related to the tone of the book?" The teacher-facilitator questions the group in order to provoke more thoughtful discussion.

"Oh, well, um, the author wanted to show the reader how the fever was taking over," Christy answers.

"And, no one was safe from this sickness," Caroline adds.

"Yeah, because the author needed to give Mattie a struggle in order to make the fever more personal," Justin states.

"This makes the reader feel sad for Matilda and makes you want to keep reading to see if her mom will survive," Luke finally says.

Yes! This is the meaningful discussion you have your students strive for from the beginning.

If you had to dream of the perfect student-centered interaction, this moment would be it! You see the success of literacy groups and you feel a sense of pride for your students' determination to give literacy groups all they have; and, on that note, you can leave the group discussion and simply nod your head with a smile of approval and continue to observe. Now let us see how the sample student discussion continues to unfold.

"Okay, Luke. . . ." The discussion director continues to lead the group in sharing their roles from last night's reading schedule. Luke is the thoughtful connector. His job is to make different types of connections to the text in order to enhance meaning for himself and the group members.

"I'm the connector. This is from the other night. I have passed through many farms before. One time I was in a big fire and I was scared to death just like Mattie."

"You were?" Christy inquires.

"Yeah, it was very scary," Luke verifies as the thoughtful connector.

"What happened? How were you caught in the fire?" Justin inquires.

"It was a brush fire. Okay, one time at my house, when I was in my house and I was about ten and I was freaked out because I was home alone and there was a person coming to my door just like Mattie feels. And then when it gets dark, I turn my lights on because sometimes I get uncomfortable. And sometimes in basketball I take charge and become a leader like the other day." Luke honestly shares a personal connection to the text.

When you notice that a student does not provide enough details, you will need to step in to assist with the group discussion, as in this case.

This teacher-group interaction can look like the following sample dialogue:

"You made a lot of text-to-self connections, Luke, but I would have loved more details pertaining to your memories. The details are important to help paint the connection for the group members," the teacher-facilitator explains to Luke before the group moves on to the next person.

If this were truly your class, you would also need to make a mental note to revisit the theme of making connections or whatever skill or idea was not fully developed by your students, in order to help them master it for future use.

Thus, literacy groups will help you informally test the students' abilities to utilize skills and strategies taught throughout the year in your class, which will help you focus and alter your whole-group instruction from week to week.

"Okay, Justin." The discussion director next calls on the literary luminary. His job is to highlight parts of the text that he wants the group to revisit.

"I'm literary luminary, and this one is the one from yesterday. I did page 154, and I like the whole entire page because it had the prayer where they were burying the person. So, let's all turn to page

154." In this role, Justin leads the group to a part in the text to be reread aloud.

"I'll read!" Christy volunteers enthusiastically. *"I spoke slowly, with iron force behind every word . . ."* She reads the entire page from *Fever 1793*, by Laurie Halse Anderson (2000).

"So, why did you pick that passage? Because I don't know," Caroline says.

"Because I thought it was kind of powerful the way she, like right here: 'I spoke slowly with an iron force.' This shows the importance of the death to the author and the reader," Justin explains.

Remember, opportunities will arise for you to truly push your students to the ultimate limit of their cognitive ability, and this is one of those moments. Watch and see how this teacher takes advantage of the current discussion within the sample dialogue. "What do you think it means—'I spoke slowly with an iron force'?" the teacher questions, hoping to help the group dig a little deeper into the author's words.

"She was upset," Caroline answers.

"No, she was angry with frustration," Justin declares.

"What do you mean, Justin?" the teacher asks curiously, probing for more.

"Well, um . . . the author wants the reader to know—no, *understand* she is demanding the burying to be her way, but she is also sad to lose her grandfather," he adds for clarification. The teacher shakes her head up and down and smiles because these students are truly reading and interacting with the text.

The facilitator challenges, "How can you prove your point using the text as your support?"

"Um, like . . . the word 'slowly' tells me she is saddened by the death, but the word 'iron force' tells me she feels strong about her meaning," Justin elaborates.

Wow! That is all you can say as your students reach that higher level of thinking. You are truly speechless at their success in reading to learn. This is what teaching is all about!

It is your dream to empower every student with the ability and desire to be a good reader for learning different forms of content, and literacy groups will help that dream come to life in your classroom! Let us observe how all of this great interaction comes to a closing point.

"Okay, now we need to discuss *what if . . .*" Christy directs the group to move on to the next of the literacy groups' goals.

"What if, um, the fever never started?" Caroline starts out.

"Then this whole book would be totally different and her mom wouldn't have gotten sick," Christy retorts.

"It wouldn't be interesting; there would be no reason to read it and the title would be pointless," they all agree.

"What if the people didn't find Matilda and she was still out there and everything?" Christy offers to the group.

"It would be hard for her to live because she couldn't take care of herself and Nell, the baby. Plus, she might have died," Caroline points out.

"What if she didn't find the stream and the pears?" Christy brings another point up for discussion.

"She wouldn't have been able to eat and struggled much more and maybe been more likely to get the fever," Luke states.

"Okay, I have one more. What if Matilda never knew her mom was alive? What do you think she would be thinking? Do you think she would go find her?" Caroline asks.

"She would be really sad and have less of a reason to keep going," Justin offers as an answer.

"Okay, Luke, your turn," Christy directs.

"What if, um, they don't survive crossing the Delaware?" Luke inquires.

"Um, then they don't survive; they die!" Justin quickly points out the obvious.

Christy concurs. "Basically!"

"Then the book would end!" Caroline points out.

Justin asks, "What if Matilda changes her mind, instead of going home and taking care of herself that she goes to the orphan house?"

"I think she should go to the orphan house because she can get food and water. Okay, I have two questions. One thing is, do you think Eliza will let her stay with her, and do you think Matilda will go to the orphan house to just drop Nell off, and then she's not going to stay? I think that's what she's going to do." Caroline's speech is half question and half prediction.

Christy offers her opinion: "She might stay for a little to get food and water and then leave because she is strong willed and has a plan."

"Okay, now we should read together. We should start on page 175." Caroline continues to move the group through the literacy goals for the day.

"*Eliza watched Nell sleeping,*" Christy reads aloud to the group as they follow along. When she no longer wants to read, she says "popcorn" and chooses another group member to pick up where she leaves off, so everyone is encouraged to follow along.

"Guys, we have to wrap it up! We're out of time," Caroline reminds the group at the conclusion of the allotted block of time written on the board.

You will need to monitor the time even though you have the discussion director doing it because you will need to pull the class back together to debrief about how literacy groups unfolded during the class time.

"Good discussion today, groups. Think about what has been said when you are reading tonight," the teacher states.

Be sure to ask one person from each group to share a success and one improvement to the entire class before you dismiss them. Ask the students how their group's text is connected to the overall class theme being taught in whole-class lecture, the course textbook, and independent practice time. Then have students return to their seats for dismissal.

"Okay, class. That's a wrap for today. I heard quite a bit of productive conversation amongst the groups today. Remember to finish your last reading schedule day and complete your literacy role. Final projects, which you chose yesterday, are due on Monday, so don't forget. I will work with table 1 tomorrow unless there is a group that runs into any confusion tonight during reading. Okay, you are free to go and have a great day!"

Thus, another day of literacy groups comes to a conclusion, and students exit your classroom with a little more understanding of the novel, chapter, or article they read and a bit more empowered to be lifelong independent learners.

As the students exit the classroom, you will not be able to help but smile at the conversation that will still occur among them. In some cases a student has paired up with someone from a different literacy group to basically give a "book talk" and promote his or her own group's awesome book!

Kylene Beers, author of *When Kids Can't Read: What Teachers Can Do* (2003), defines this type of discussion as not necessarily giving a synopsis of the book, but rather attempting to entice others into wanting to read the book. Literacy groups create this type of desire. They allow students to explore learning through multiple types of text and broaden their understanding of your content area.

"They were whipped until they started bleeding!" one young boy shares a small piece of information he learned from the book *The Narrative Life of Fredrick Douglass* (2004) with his friend from another group.

The other kid questions with disbelief, "Really?"

You will even overhear the students talking about their books as they walk to lunch with their friends from other periods. They are telling them what books to choose when certain choices come around. "You have to choose *Tears of a Tiger* [by Sharon Draper] when it is offered to your class because it holds your attention the entire time and it's exciting but sad too!" Now this is a reading community on fire!

This is what it is all about: students reading, learning from, and thinking about all kinds of different texts while enjoying them to the point of gossiping about the titles with their friends! Thus, each year you will get a little closer to building a community of readers.

Even your students will see the benefits of literacy groups. As Steven states, "I think that literacy groups are a great idea because it helps you get to know your classmates better and can help you understand books better. It's also great because we can choose a book to read and it can help you see who likes your types of books. When you choose your role, you can express yourself through it, so I think that is awesome!"

"Yeah," Nathan interjects. "I think literacy groups are a good way to get to know your other classmates and new books too. In literacy groups you get to pick the text you want and you have to read a certain number of pages a day which keeps you organized. It is the best kind of group learning I've ever been in; it is fun but you still have to work. I like how the best group of the day gets to sit in the comfy chairs the next day!"

WHAT YOU HAVE LEARNED ABOUT LITERACY IN ACTION

Due to the fact that few professional-development trainings in secondary strategies are provided, secondary educators are sometimes left in the shadows of their own devices—because all the energy and effort is put into elementary education.

Oftentimes, teachers go without answers and are expected to help students continue to make gains in their reading without the proper resources, such as money.

In addition, content-area teachers are asked to incorporate reading instruction into their already packed agendas. With reading as the foundation of all other areas of learning, you would expect more. How can we maintain consistency without proper guidelines? Easy—implement literacy groups to create that student-centered classroom!

Also, why is there such a large gap when it comes to supporting secondary teachers in using solid reading strategies and interaction to makes gains for all students? It should not be this way, and, as educators, we believe that all students are capable of making gains, learning and mastering new material and skills, and overcoming new challenges!

This means we need to step out of that old saying, "It's not my job to teach students to read," and come to the realization that we are all responsible for every student's journey through our educational doors, whether those doors lead through science, math, or social studies.

Of course, that is why you have chosen to read this professional text on using literacy groups to enhance your students' achievement gains within your subject area.

The student interaction that you just read took months to build and maintain. However, with proper guidance and support, it can be accomplished faster. It is for this reason that you have been provided with the chapters to come.

You can take the scenario you just read and allow it to help you develop your own literacy strategies. You will build a systematic approach to literacy groups that will bring your students joy in reading to learn your content! Your students will excel in your subject because you empowered them!

In the chapters to come, you will explore this exciting way of learning through literacy groups. You will learn what it means to use literacy groups and see the many oversights that can be made while using the process with your secondary students, as well as the steps you can take to be as successful as possible.

So sit back with a cup of tea or coffee and prepare to take a journey through literacy groups at the secondary school level. It is a journey worth taking! After all, Ashley, like many students sitting in your classroom right now, seems to think so: "I think literacy groups are fun because it gives me the chance to read new books and then hear people's opinions on the books."

2

Understanding Literacy Groups

"I think literacy groups are cool because you see a lot of books, and it gives you a chance to understand the book. Plus you can hear other opinions, and now I like books when I used to hate books." (Michael shares his feelings about literacy groups.)

You never know what students think until you ask them. So ask and listen, but most of all, don't be afraid to try something new! This chapter will help you feel more comfortable with the idea of literacy groups in terms of what it means and why it proves to be a solid approach to cooperative literacy learning. As you read this chapter, keep in mind the big picture developed for you in chapter 1.

Every teacher can relate to sitting in a Friday-morning meeting with the rest of the faculty, taking in a presentation on high-stakes standardized-testing scores from the year before.

Suddenly, your attention has drifted off to daydream about all of your students passing this high-stakes standardized test due to the use of literacy groups combined with whole-class instruction! As if literacy groups were an original idea and created a "fix all" teaching program!

You cannot help but smile to yourself and refocus your attention on the administrator speaking: "We need to provide differentiated instruction in order to meet the diverse needs of our students so that we can get our scores up for this year. Work with your teams or other teachers in your department to create a plan of action. Students need to be reading to learn, and it's your job to get them there!"

"Good, I'm not the only one thinking we can solve the educational gap that exists with one big great idea!" you think to yourself as the meeting comes to an end.

Then, as you leave the meeting, another teacher comes up to speak with you. He is a respected colleague, and you oftentimes engage in repartee. Since you have a friendship, you both feel comfortable expressing your opinions with each other. He is just really easygoing, and you have camaraderie after working together for several years, and so you feel comfortable challenging him as a professional after such a presentation.

"What do you think of changing the way you teach for each student to be a better reader in your subject area?" you openly ask him as you walk out of the morning meeting together.

"I don't have time to teach each student how to read my content material. They should have learned that in elementary school," this veteran teacher shares with you.

"What about having them learn the same information, but in different ways within small groups or individualized research projects?" you suggest.

"That's absurd! I teach middle school, not elementary, and I don't have time for centers, nor do I have time to grade 130 students' research projects of regurgitated halfhearted content. Besides, they have a textbook with plenty of good information in it," he states adamantly.

With some concern, you ask, "Really? What do you do for students who have a difficult time reading to learn from the textbook because the text is too difficult, or who tend to be withdrawn from learning because they are bored?"

"I tell them to read it again and get over it; it's their job to learn information that teachers present to them," he says in a matter-of-fact manner.

"How's that working for you?" you ask with extreme curiosity and a bit of sarcasm.

"I have been using the same method of teaching for my entire career and it works just fine, so why should I try something new? I don't hear students complaining, so there's no problem," he says as the conversation concludes and he walks away with a heavy foot.

Unfortunately, his students have stated out of the blue to you several times throughout the school year how bored they are in his class: "All we do is read a chapter and answer questions."

You tell them, "Every teacher has his or her own method of teaching," because you do not want to support students' negative comments about other teachers.

The sad truth is, every adult can recall learning in such a manner at some point in his or her educational career. For example, think back to when you were in middle school and you had that one teacher—maybe even a huge man who looked like he really belonged more on a football field than in a classroom, or an ancient-looking, gray-haired women who should have retired decades ago. You remember!

You would walk into the classroom to find the assignment written on the board: "Read chapter 3 and answer the questions at the end of the chapter. Answers are due at the end of class."

When the late bell rings, the teacher stands at the front of the class for a brief moment, reads the assignment already written on the board, and sits down at his desk. You are not sure what he does at his desk, but you know not to bother him for any reason. You also know you never read fast enough to get the entire chapter read and answer the questions.

Unfortunately, this feeling and this anxiety are quite common among struggling learners/readers. You look around and see all the other students busily working on the questions, after what seems like only a few minutes of class have gone by. You get extremely worried, so you stop reading and start to try to answer the questions.

Sadly, you don't understand what you read in the first place, so skimming for answers is like trying to swim with a weight attached to your waist. You constantly watch the clock because you want to do well in school; you just have a difficult time reading the textbook.

The end of the period comes, and all you have to turn in is a piece of notebook paper with your name, the date, the period, the heading, and the phrase "question 1" written on it. You feel defeated again, due to your lack of ability to play the textbook game! Can you relate? Better yet, can your students relate?

Consequently, you never earned anything higher than a D in any class similar to the one just described, solely because the textbook was your only option for learning the content, and it was beyond your cognitive ability. Over the years, this type of teaching only pushed you further through the cracks of education.

There is hope! The twenty-first century has brought much reform to education, examples of which include the No Child Left Behind Act of 2001 and *Learning Focused Solutions* by Max Thompson (2005). Thus, as educators, we hope to close the achievement gap by using these best practices, such as literacy groups (*student-centered learning*).

With self-reflection and growth an important part of our profession, a powerful statement comes to mind: Teachers who continue to teach the same way and are unaware of any other approach is one thing, but teachers who know there are other ways, but refuse to try them, that's malpractice! It is a strong statement, but it may have a level of honesty that makes you think.

This is the key reminder, however, of why this professional text is so important to educators: It supports your time spent reading it and trying something different.

Therefore, we like to think that, for the most part, most teachers want students to read to learn new information and truly understand and apply it, which means reading with a critical eye and questioning the information presented in a fun and interesting manner.

In addition, most teachers want students to enjoy reading to learn new information. How do teachers turn this desire into a reality and get students to achieve both enjoyment and reading to learn? Do you want students fired up about learning your content area?

After each year, you are ready for a change from using one novel or textbook to instruct the whole class, particularly because it takes too long to complete a novel or a chapter in a textbook for five or six different classes. This is where literacy groups come in handy!

Oftentimes you will hear students complain that they want a say in the material they have to use for instruction; in other words, they want student choice. Plus, they are tired of using the same reading series where the teacher teaches and the students listen, followed by practice, questions, and assessments—after which the process is repeated for the following story or chapter!

Can you blame them for being bored? Through this professional learning opportunity you have opened your mind to grow and change with the use of literacy with your subject. You are not afraid to try something new, so you can pat yourself on the back for being a part of helping your students become well-rounded, independent individuals who are capable of functioning within society.

LITERACY GROUPS CHARACTERIZED

You guessed it: literacy groups are the answer to all of those questions! Since your passion for teaching lies within reading, writing, and researching the best approaches to deliver your content, you cannot help but to delve directly into the questions brought up by your desire to want more for your students and yourself—because the bottom line is that your students want to enjoy learning, and you want a challenge!

Let's face it: reading from a manual works, but it is easy and can be boring, and you want to utilize your professionalism to create and design something better for your students and yourself! That is why you have chosen to read this book and implement literacy groups.

As the new school year or quarter approaches, you begin to think about your options. You can continue to use the same novel with each class or the same method of delivering information solely from a textbook, but that will still take up loads of time, and students will get bored with the book or a chapter from a textbook they never chose to read to begin with. You want more for your students!

Well, so do highly respected researchers such as Richard Allington, who spoke about empowering students to learn, and teaching them the best ways possible with best practices—rather than drill and practice—at the 2007 Pasco County (Florida) Summer Literacy Institute. Literacy groups directly support his suggestion that we empower students to learn through the use of multicultural texts and materials from a variety of sources.

There are also several professional titles by other revered researchers that support the instructional practice of literacy strategies to empower students for reading, writing, and thinking across the curriculum. These are cited in the reference section.

Literacy groups have been shown to provide a student-centered classroom environment that includes authentic discussion, high engagement, written response, and on-task reading-to-learn time. This learning environment expands the possibility of student interpretation of text and ownership of learning.

The teacher is simply a facilitator who guides groups that are experiencing difficulty with quality discussion, or who helps expand or clarify understanding of difficult text (which is also an excellent opportunity to model authentic discussion). Finally, this teaching method builds collaboration, new ways to view text, and higher-order thinking about a wide range of text.

This will bring you, the teaching professional, to ponder two major points. First of all, you know this is not going to be easy to construct and put together—but is anything worth having easily obtained? Second, you cannot help but wonder if your students will actually get more out of this type of literacy instruction than they have reaped in the past from whole-group novels or lectures.

Finally, a realization comes to you like a flash of lightning! You can use a few different books, articles, or informational texts at different reading levels for students to read in groups of four or five; and you can focus daily lessons on literal and critical comprehension skills and strategies, and on concepts to assist with group discussion and comprehension at different cognitive levels.

The use of literacy groups in your content area will also lend itself to differentiated instruction and student choice, which will increase students' desires to read and learn in a collaborative way.

Of course, then you may decide that you want the books or articles to be connected by topic, idea, theme, or concept, to go along with your learning objectives, and that you want a mix of fiction and nonfiction high-interest texts in order to build a well-rounded perspective. That way, students will learn all the same ideas but through the eyes of different texts.

Plus, you know you will need different reading levels and different lengths as well, to help students build stamina. You do not want any student to feel left out or frustrated during the process of reading to learn in your class, so all of these considerations are important.

Several veteran teachers and reading experts agree that most books or articles can be read in a short period of time, following the idea that students will need to read in school and at home. So you will need to look at the school-year calendar to determine how many weeks the students are in school. Then you will need to subtract three weeks at the beginning, two weeks at the end, and two weeks for standardized testing for your school.

This will lead you to figure out that you can have the students read a new novel or informational text every one to two weeks, totaling about fifteen novels or thirty articles for the entire school year. Keep in mind that short texts such as articles will only take one week to read, dissect, discuss, and draw conclusions from.

However, the work is not done yet! You still have to determine how you will ensure they actually read the novels or informational texts and understand what they read.

Plus, you will need to monitor your students' reading, guide them regularly, and assess their overall knowledge of the text. How can you accomplish all this in a secondary classroom with only fifty to ninety minutes, four to five times a week, depending on your school's bell schedule?

Yes, you know it—literacy groups! Remember, this is not a new idea, but it is a new practice for you, so keep in mind the big picture from chapter 1 as you continue reading the next part of this chapter.

Let's look into this newfound idea, literacy groups, a little further. You realize by now that everything in education seems to have a different meaning, or can be interpreted or adapted in several ways based on whom you ask, when you ask, and in what context you ask it. Literacy groups are no exception to the rule.

This leads us to discover some of the different meanings for the use of literacy groups. For example, Gipe (2006) finds similarities between book clubs and literacy groups. The latter include an account-ability factor through specific roles for each student.

Harvey and Goudvis (2000) take it further, describing literacy groups as a group opportunity where students read similar text and meet to discuss and respond to it together in a cooperative learning arrangement. This atmosphere provides students with the opportunity to ask questions, make connections, and talk about the similarities and differences between the themes.

Similarly, Keene and Zimmermann (1997) highly support this learning process and recommend it as a good strategy for helping students dig deeper into understanding text.

Even the Internet has some information pertaining to literacy groups. For example, simply Google the term "literature circles" to learn there is an abundance of agreement that characterizes literature circles as student-centered learning for a small group of four to six students, acceptable for any grade level. In the small groups, each student is required to fulfill a role in order to help lead the group in a meaningful discussion about the required text.

Furthermore, literacy groups offer an atmosphere in which students can take ownership of their own learning. They are able to share thoughts and concerns, as well as their understanding of the events of the text, with a group of peers.

Therefore, literacy groups offer a safe environment for students to learn and experiment with group discussion, which enhances the meaning of text and enriches the interest of reading to learn in all classes. Katie, a student, concurs: "I think that literacy groups are an invigorating experience. To me, it helps me understand more of what the author is implying or stating in the book or novel."

Another student, Kathryn, agrees: "I think literacy roles are helpful to people because just in case they don't get the book, we do things in class, like summarize and question to help us understand the book, and also get to talk with the other kids about why they like the book."

HISTORICAL IMPRESSION

For a concept that is sweeping the nation (and also sweeping across some other countries, such as Japan), literacy groups are not new to the world of learning. The topic has appeared in articles, journals, work-shops, and books. It is used at all grade levels, with varying degrees of intricacy. The teaching method has actually been around for about twenty-six years.

In fact, literacy groups (also known as *literature circles, book clubs*, etc.), were originally implemented as an idea by an elementary teacher, Karen Smith of Phoenix, Arizona, who needed to instruct students in reading but only had a few mismatched book sets. Thus was born a wonderful creation. Over the years, additional components have been added to the literacy-group practice to make it more rewarding and challenging for the students.

Much research has occurred on the effectiveness of this teaching method over the years. Some of the leading researchers include Schlick Noe (1999); Hill, Johnson, and Schlick Noe (1995, 2001, 2003); Johnson (1999); and Daniels (1994, 2002, 2004).

The research concludes that student interaction within groups has proven effective in digging deeper into the author's meaning. This growth is attributed to the teacher stepping back as the leader, allowing the students to take the lead in their own learning.

However, the teacher is not completely removed from the big picture, because his or her ability to scaffold and coach the student-centered learning is crucial to helping all students be active participants within literacy groups.

WHAT YOU HAVE LEARNED TO SUPPORT
THE USE OF LITERACY GROUPS

In conclusion, you now have a foundation of what it means to implement literacy groups and an understanding of what it means to conduct literacy groups with teacher guidance.

Unfortunately, reading about something, seeing it, and doing it yourself are completely different! This is where having the support and guidance of this professional book will truly come in handy.

All you need to do now is learn how to develop a detailed plan for organizing the process; decide how the students will be involved in the process; decide what literacy roles will look like; learn how the daily lessons will assist the groups with understanding; and determine how you will assess their understanding of the different forms of texts. You are off and running!

In the next chapter, you will learn how to organize text into categories in order to design a foundation for implementing literacy groups, which will be no easy task! It will open your eyes to an endless range of possibilities for using literacy groups in any classroom setting and with any subject area, as well as with several forms of text. So get up and stretch, but don't wander too far—because it is about to get descriptive!

3

Designing Literacy Groups

"I think that literacy groups are a good way for students to interact and talk about something educational. It helps us understand reading strategies," Leslie expresses after experiencing this teaching method.

Every journey needs leaders and followers, and literacy groups are no exception. Whether you work with a team of teachers or on a task force, when you have an idea that you want others to jump on board with, you have to sell your idea in the most appealing way.

Being the leader of your classroom, you have to be enthusiastic about your lessons in order to motivate your students to willingly interact with and learn from your method or approach to teaching the concept for the day. This way, you know you have a support system as you venture out into the land of learning groups.

ESTABLISHING SUITABLE COMBINATIONS

Once you obtain your students' support for giving literacy groups a try, you are ready to begin the grouping process. You should start out the way any "elementary" teacher would, assessing your students in order to determine each one's individual reading ability/level and strengths/limitations.

Assessing individual needs will give the student a good idea of where he or she will start, and it will help you plan small-group instruction based on individual needs. There are many diagnostic tools available for accomplishing the task. It will take some time, but it is well worth the effort.

One method of assessment is to use a *running record*. Running records assess the student's fluency, comprehension, word-attack skills, and self-correction capabilities. You can actually get a lot of data from a ten- to fifteen-minute assessment.

A running record is kept as a student reads out loud. The teacher uses check marks to signify a correctly read word and a mark for errors (McCormick, 2003) to indicate omissions, self-corrections, rereads, and so on.

Then the student answers a series of questions pertaining to the reading. In order for the results to equal an *instructional level* (a teacher-guided level), the student should read with more than 90 percent accuracy and score 75 percent or higher on the comprehension. That is the ideal place for students in order to read at a level where learning occurs with teacher assistance but very little frustration.

A running record can be any short text with questions to check comprehension and text difficulty, or you can locate leveled text online for the sole purpose of administering running records. For example, *Reading A–Z* (www.readinga-z.com) provides this assessment for members.

Another method of assessment is to use the Analytical Reading Inventory (ARI). This is similar to a running record; however, it provides a little more depth.

First you build rapport with the student by explaining the process. Then you conduct a reading interview in order to determine the student's reading interests, attitudes, habits, and perceptions about reading, as well as the strategies he or she uses with reading; this is followed by having the student read orally from a leveled word list, which identifies the student's text-level ability.

Next, the student reads the leveled passage while you assess prior knowledge and application of reading strategies. Finally, you code miscues, check fluency, monitor the student's ability to retell, ask comprehension questions, and score the data.

The second part of using this in-depth diagnostic tool is determining the student's silent-reading ability. This is where the student reads leveled text to him- or herself and answers questions about the text. In most cases the student is able to read and comprehend at a higher level with silent reading versus oral reading.

Then you will determine the student's listening-comprehension level. This is where you read a passage aloud and ask the student questions about the text. The final stage is to assess the student's reading level for expository passages. When each portion of the diagnostic is complete, you will summarize the results and determine a plan of action.

Keep in mind that this method of assessment takes thirty to forty minutes, but it provides much more information about the student. There is a book package that will walk you through the entire process and allow you to practice before using the ARI with your students: *Analytical Reading Inventory: Comprehensive Assessment for All Students Including Gifted and Remedial*, by Mary Lynn Woods and Alden J. Moe (2003).

For students about whom you may have deeper concerns, you can use an assessment that takes forty-five to sixty minutes, *Diagnostic Assessment of Reading*, by Florence G. Roswell et al. (2005). The assessment evaluates limitations and strengths in reading, writing, and language. It can be used for any student from kindergarten to high school.

The Diagnostic Assessment of Reading is made up of nine tests: Print Awareness, Phonological Awareness, Letters and Sounds, Word Recognition, Word Analysis, Oral Reading, Silent Reading Comprehension, Spelling, and Word Meaning. This tool provides a teacher's manual that walks you through each test and tells you how to score and summarize the information.

However, the reading specialist or literacy leader at your school usually administers this diagnostic, so check into it before you make the investment yourself.

After you identify each student's reading level (strengths and limitations), you will place four to five students into one group based on their levels, interests, personalities, and social-interaction abilities.

You need to consider the dynamics of each group. For example, to group your students only by reading level is solely *homogeneous grouping*, where the students read a text on their instructional level (also known as their *zone of proximal development*).

The *instructional level* is where students are capable of reading most of the book but need teacher assistance to reach a higher level of understanding, to think critically beyond the text. However, this type of grouping will cause misbehavior because you will have all the struggling readers in one group (Vacca and Vacca, 2005).

Therefore, this is not exactly the best type of grouping for your secondary students. Rather, you will want a more independent and student-centered learning process, for which a *heterogeneous grouping* is ideal.

For that reason, once the students get used to this method of group learning, you can reassign the students so that there is a student from each level represented in each group, or you can vary the assignments from the beginning.

For example, if you have twenty-five students and five different reading levels that range from third-grade to ninth-grade ability, you can place one level 3 with one student each from levels 4, 5, 6, and 7, in order to make a more well-rounded group that is more likely to produce higher-level thinking, greater productivity, and more discussion.

Another group can consist of one level 6 paired with two level 7s, one level 8, and one level 9. The most important rule to remember is to keep the levels close to each other, so do not place a level 9 with a level 3. Think about grouping your highest student with a medium-low student, and your medium-high student with a low student.

However you choose to approach grouping, it will take patience and time to get to this desirable destination, but you should embark on the journey anyway, no longer blind and unaware of the bumps and blocks along the way!

If what you know now, you knew at the beginning of your teaching career, you could have saved yourself from hitting many potholes. But then what would you have to smile about when you look back today while reading this book and learning about a new method of teaching for your content area?

The students remind us what literacy groups are all about and remind us of the reason all the hard work is worth it. It is the encouragement from the students that keeps us growing and learning each year!

"I think literacy groups are very beneficial for us because it gives us a chance to work with different kids who all like the same book. Plus, working in small groups allows us to share likes and dislikes about the book and to see it from different perspectives. I also like literacy roles which go hand in hand with literacy groups because it encourages us to discuss what's happening in the book," Amy, a student, shares.

IDENTIFYING TEXT

When you finish establishing student groups, you are ready to determine what text to use in order to guide learning and discussion for the class.

Unfortunately, some students do not remember reading any books during their time in elementary or middle school. How sad is that? Other students remember being read to by a teacher.

For example, one student recalls her third-grade teacher picking up the book *My Teacher Is an Alien*, by Bruce Coville (1989), at the end of every day and reading a chapter aloud. "The way he read and stopped to add in his own thoughts captured my attention," the student shares. Then there are students who do not have their first memory of reading a book until later in high school.

Sadly, a few reading experiences occur when students are required to read books such as *Snow Falling on Cedars*, by David Guterson (1995), and *The Scarlet Letter*, by Nathaniel Hawthorne (1959), in which they struggle through every word. Oftentimes those students become frustrated and give up, which ends with the book being thrown across the room and tears flowing heavily down their cheeks, or with the students acting out in class to avoid the real problem.

In some cases, an undesirable text does not receive the proper support from the teacher. The teacher simply has the students read assigned pages at home and come to class and talk about what they've read, which struggling learners cannot do since they do not finish the assigned reading. Then the teacher gives a test on the text, which struggling learners do poorly on since they have no clue what the text is truly about.

Looking back now, do you know where your struggling readers are coming from? They do not comprehend what they read, and they have much difficulty with the vocabulary used throughout the text, nor do they care about the content. They feel no connection to the text. In addition, they have been struggling readers their entire schooling careers, so this situation has only added to their hatred for reading and built the barrier higher.

Luckily, this hatred can end if students discover the perfect book. One former struggling reader recounts his climb over the barrier of hatred for reading when he found a book about the Holocaust: "I found it in the hallway one early morning before school was to start. This book was the first book where I felt connected to the text. I read that book, *Daniel's Story*, by Carol Matas [1993], from cover to end, and when I was finished, I picked up another book about the Holocaust and read it too."

Fortunately, this antireader learned he did not hate all books; he truly enjoyed reading about adversity from history because he could relate it to the hard times he was going through at home. It made him feel his life was not so bad compared to the former.

In addition, he realized that the more he read, the better he got at it! Of course, he still had difficulty attacking unfamiliar words, but he was reading by choice now, so he ignored what seemed to be unimportant to him at the time. His reading continued, and that is why he is on his way to college today; his struggles became his motivation to always learn and try new things!

Thus it is through weaknesses that one is led to greatness. In this case, difficulties inspire strengths to reach out to other in order to guide them to find the same success discovered through learning to read. This student is the reason teachers try so hard! Think about why you became a teacher of your subject area, and how reading this professional-development text about literacy groups will help you inspire those you teach.

This desire to help students find the joys in reading to learn gives teachers the willingness to always read, research, and write, which is why you are reading this text.

Many teachers take on a lot each school year. Most teachers tend to get to work earlier than contracted, such as at the start of summer. Even the week before teacher planning, teachers are at the school giving up much of their personal time to pull their classrooms together just to start the year off clean and fresh. What do teachers end up stepping into?

Then again, teachers are fueled by the desire to help students become the best they can be, and literacy groups can assist with that goal!

The first step is to take an inventory of your classroom library collection to determine what titles you have multiple copies of already.

Then you should get with the media specialist at your school to determine what class sets are currently stored for teacher checkout, as well as what titles are available on the school media shelves with multiple copies for checkout. You will want four to five copies of each title.

Luckily, there are several titles to choose from that relate to social studies as well as other subjects, such as *Bud, Not Buddy*, by Christopher Paul Curtis (1999); *Number the Stars*, by Lois Lowry (1989); and *The Red Badge of Courage*, by Stephen Crane (1983), just to name a few.

You will also want to search newspapers, magazines, and online articles. This will expand the students' reading experiences, which will add to their ability to comprehend the textbook. Peruse the newspaper daily and start saving interesting articles in a folder. You can even get articles from newspapers of other cities and states by getting onto their websites. Do the same with magazines.

You can even ask your faculty to donate magazines or purchase a subscription to one you will get multiple uses out of, such as *Junior*

Scholastic. Also, do not forget that the Internet offers an abundance of resources, but be sure to check the authorship, the domain (.com, .net, .edu, .gov, or .org), and the accuracy of the information prior to using it.

Next, you will need to read the synopses on the back covers of the books to determine what the books are mostly about. Also, read the other forms of text in their entirety. You do not want to limit students' choices to only text you have read, so you should explore all possible options and get familiar with a broad range of text, as well as sources. This will help ensure that you have plenty to choose from for each concept or topic throughout the year.

You can also read some of the texts right alongside the students, in order to expand your own knowledge. Now, go search and find several titles in a wide range of text!

GROUPING TEXT

Finally, you should group the titles by common topics or themes. This will allow the discussion among the students to be meaningful and connected.

For example, *Harriet Tubman*, by Ann Petry (1955); *Roll of Thunder, Hear My Cry*, by Mildred Taylor (2002); *Anne Frank: The Diary of a Young Girl* (the abridged and adapted version prepared by Mark Falstein; 1995); *Narrative of the Life of Frederick Douglass* (written by Douglass; 2004); and *Under the Same Sky*, by Cynthia DeFelice (2003) all represent human struggle against oppression based on race, ethnicity, or nationality. (See appendix A for the entire book list.)

In addition, the group of texts described above represents an array of genres, such as nonfiction, realistic fiction, and autobiography, as well as different reading levels. The titles also vary in difficulty, and they vary in length as well; yet all students are learning the same concept. This is an excellent way to implement differentiated instruction!

For example, the group of books mentioned above ranges from intermediate level (grades 3–5) for *Anne Frank* (with only 92 pages); to right on grade level (grade 6) for *Under the Same Sky* (with 215 pages); to upper-middle level (grades 7–8) for *Roll of Thunder, Hear My Cry* (with 210 pages).

Also, a variety of genres are selected to provide students with the necessary exposure to help them become proficient readers in any situation.

Harvey (1998) confirms the importance of reading a wide range of text: when students practice reading nonfiction text, they are also improving higher-order critical skills, such as research and analysis. This leads to higher-order thinking and deeper discussion among peers, which is what must occur for true learning to be represented!

Furthermore, reading levels can be determined by using some form of a reliable and valid reading text assessment, such as the Lexile Framework for Reading created by MetaMetrics (www.lexile.com/EntrancePageHtml.aspx?1).

This is a website that provides educators, parents, and researchers with information on thousands of titles, such as reading levels, assessments, and additional resources and/or tools.

For example, in order for sixth-grade students to be considered within grade level, based on this source, students must be able to read books leveled from 800 to 1050. These scores are determined by length, text complexity, *syntax* (sentence structure) and *semantics* (interrelationships of words, phrases, and sentences), and content vocabulary.

Students obtain their scores by taking the Scholastic Reading Inventory (SRI) at the beginning, middle, and end of the school year. This way, students do not need to feel pain and struggle when participating in literacy groups, since the texts vary in complexity and length.

It also helps slower readers choose shorter books, such as *Sadako and the Thousand Paper Cranes,* by Eleanor Coerr (1977), or *Ben and Me: An Astonishing Life of Benjamin Franklin by His Good Mouse Amos,* by Robert Lawson (1988); while faster readers choose longer and more difficult novels, such as *The Scarlet Letter,* by Nathaniel Hawthorne (2007), or *Night,* by Elie Wiesel (2006).

Please note that a short text can be just as difficult as a longer one. However, all students are encouraged to challenge themselves by selecting something more difficult each time, either by selecting a new genre, a higher level (within 100 points), or a greater number of pages. If you do not have access to SRI, then you can determine students' levels through alternative methods.

One easy and quick way to measure if a book is too difficult for a student is to use the five-finger rule. This is where the student simply turns to any random page in the desired book and reads that page. If the student comes across five unfamiliar words, then the book is too difficult.

Another way to determine a student's reading ability is to administer a running record (explained previously in this chapter), which can be taken directly from books, chapters, articles, magazines, and other sources.

You can give every student a grade-level vocabulary test, such as the Word Opposites Test. This is where students receive groups of ten words, starting at the first-grade level, and they are asked to identify the word that means the opposite or nearly the opposite of the numbered word. They continue to work through each group until they become frustrated, guess too much, or just decide they do not know the words in the group.

The vocabulary groups go up to high-school level, so this method serves as a good indicator to determine a starting point for reading. The last group of ten words on which the student earns a 70 percent score or higher is the student's identified level. Finally, you can always access reading assessments online, such as Reading A–Z and Study Island.

It will not be an easy task to create categories, locate texts, and organize it all, but it is all worth it. Carson agrees: "I think literacy groups and roles are a great way to read. It is great to share what you think about the book with others."

ROTATING TEXT MATERIAL

Now you are ready to determine the rotation of the text sets for each class. Start with the first set of texts, which consists of four groups of five titles each, for a total of twenty text choices.

Then create a chart with one column for the title, one column for the author, one for the genre, one for the number of pages, and one for the reading level. You will use this information to present text options to the class so they can make an informed decision as to what title they want to read and enjoy.

Table 3.1 is an excerpt from the book list provided in the appendix as an example. You will rotate the groups of books not only within a class but also among several classes, since in this example there are four classes involved in the rotation process. If you teach five classes, you will need to come up with one additional text set of five copies for each rotation.

The rotation of the text sets is the most challenging part, because you cannot immediately use the books coming in (just in case students do not return them the day they are due), and so you have to use the next set of twenty books.

For this example, you will notice there are a total of four sets of twenty titles, for a total of eighty titles to use with four classes (each of which consists of twenty-one to twenty-four students). In the example illustrated in this professional text, the text sets can accommodate a

Table 3.1. Example of Book-List Rotation

Dates	Theme	Book	Author	Genre	Pages	Lexile
3rd 9/10–23	Human	Harriet Tubman	Ann Petry	Nonfiction	242	1000
2nd 11/5–18	struggle	Roll of Thunder, Hear My Cry	Mildred Taylor	Historical Fiction	210	920
6th 1/22–2/3		Under the Same Sky	Cynthia DeFelice	Realistic Fiction	224	750
4th 5/12–25		Narrative of Life of F. Douglass	Frederick Douglass	Autobiography	122	700
5th 5/28–6/8		Anne Frank: Diary of a Young Girl	Mark Falstein	Nonfiction	92	500

total of twenty-five students; so if you have more than that, you will need to add an additional set to each group rotation.

Remember that each set of five books represents five students, which is one literacy group. You can certainly have groups of six, but you should try to keep your groups smaller because students will work better together and fewer problems will arise. Vacca and Vacca (2005) suggest that the size of the cooperative learning group should be determined by the skills needed to accomplish the learning goal.

Once you have the sets established, you will determine the classes in which each set of twenty titles will be used, and the dates. It is best to figure this out ahead of time to eliminate confusion or chaos later. The more you are organized and prepared, the smoother the process will turn out!

To illustrate: Your first class can use set 1, your second class can use set 2, your third class can use set 3, and your last class can use set 4. (Each set has five titles in it.)

They will have their text choice for two weeks, for example from September 10 to September 23. This allows them time to read in and out of class and complete their literacy role and a final project. Once they finish their text, you will move to the second group of twenty titles and use the second group in the same fashion.

However, the categories and titles are merely an example to guide you in your decision to take on literacy groups in your classroom. The reading schedule can certainly be adapted to meet the needs of any subject and classroom. You only need four to five copies of each title, and you can switch out titles and add in picture books, articles, poems, textbook chapters, and so on.

Table 3.2 is another example of text rotation, using articles instead of books. The titles provided were found using an educational search engine, go-passport.grolier.com/. You can use lit groups with any text source, including your textbook. The possibilities are endless!

Table 3.2. Text Rotation Using Online Articles

Dates	Theme	Text Titles	Sources	Genre	Pages	Lexile
Class 1		The Energy Picture	Grolier Online	Nonfiction	2	1350
Class 2		Power, Generation and Transmission	Grolier Online	Nonfiction	2	1500
Class 3	Energy	Alternative Energy Sources	Grolier Online	Nonfiction	2	1200
Class 4		The Energy Policy Act of 2005	Grolier Online	Nonfiction	1	1000
Class 5		Thermonuclear Energy	Grolier Online	Nonfiction	2	750

Moreover, in this professional text you will notice that all text examples are books, but articles, poems, and other forms of text are used with the daily lessons to promote modeling, scaffolding, and practice of comprehension strategies and skills—which is explained in the upcoming chapters. This way the students receive a variety of text in different settings for multiple purposes.

Furthermore, Donna Norton, author of *Multicultural Children's Literature: Through the Eyes of Many Children* (2005), reminds us to choose a diverse range of text to meet the cultural needs and interests of the ever-changing classroom within the American culture.

WHAT YOU HAVE LEARNED ABOUT BUILDING A LITERACY ENVIRONMENT

As your planning or prep work comes to an end and after several hours of reviewing, revising, and adjusting, you are ready to finalize the reading schedule for the school year. You should feel good to know your students will have choices when it comes to reading books or articles for your class.

Jenny confirms this feeling: "I think literacy groups are a good way to pick and read new books, and it always makes you read more because you got to choose the book."

Mark also agrees: "I think literacy groups are a great way to learn." With that being said, you are now ready to tackle the intricate details pertaining to the implementation or daily use of the texts within this literacy-group concept.

This chapter should have inspired you to take apart the chapters in your textbooks, divide the poems up by author, or tackle newspaper articles based on topic or section. Why just use the same text for all students? What does it matter if students take different roads to reach the same destination, as long as the ride to get there challenges them within their zones of proximal development?

Ultimately, the journey is just as important as the outcome! It is the process that empowers the students to be lifelong learners! And learning is the whole purpose of teaching.

As you continue your journey through literacy groups at the secondary level, you will experience firsthand how the students get started, how they work together, and how they monitor their understanding during reading. So continue to step out of your comfort zone, in order to try something that is a lot of work but that has an amazing effect on students' ability to read to learn—literacy groups!

4

Student and
Teacher Accountability

"I think literacy group roles were great. It helped me understand the book much better because just in case I don't understand something in the book, I ask one of my peers and they help me out. I give thanks for having literacy groups and roles," Brad shares at the end of class one day.

A few years ago, a couple adopted their first dog, a small, two-and-a-half-pound, all-white Chihuahua. His head was bigger than his body, so he looked like one of those bobble-head characters you see in people's car windows.

Since he was all white and small, they decided to name him Zeus, to give him big personality; but he did not need the name, because he was already big and mighty. Actually, he thought he was as big as a Great Dane.

Now, Zeus was not afraid to explore or venture out on his own, and they did not mind him building his confidence because it was hilarious to watch this tiny body carry around what seemed to be a very large head. Unfortunately, Zeus built too much confidence; he would go anywhere without thinking, which led to many casualties. One time he was stung by a wasp, and his little paw swelled up to the size of a very large cherry.

Another time, he was tackled by a wave on the beach; and if that was not enough, he also found himself challenged by a crab he'd decided to chase around the sand on the beach. He even had the courage to stick his nose into the crab's hole. Zeus constantly found himself in predicaments because he jumped into situations without evaluating the best approach.

Luckily, he was spared many times, but the next pothole was unknown with the overzealous puppy! Consequently, they laughed at his predicaments; teachers sometimes have difficulty laughing at their quandaries, especially when they are happening. They like to get it right the first time. Afterward, teachers tend to crack a smile at their mistakes because they too act spontaneously at times. Besides, teachers are human!

OVERZEALOUS OVERSIGHT

Once the reading schedule is complete, you are free to explore literacy roles and procedures. In other words, determine how the students will interact, how you will monitor their understanding, and how you will manage your time. These are extremely important points to consider for avoiding a little chaos or unexpected surprises.

This professional text will offer you guidelines on all these points and more. As a result, you will feel comfortable implementing literacy groups as a way of using text to improve reading to learn. Your students will master skills and strategies specific to your content area.

With the start of the school year, semester, or quarter, you will sit down to put together a way for students to learn how to participate productively in literacy groups. Of course, you might become overzealous at this time, due to all the different options and from the excitement of trying something new; you will end up like a Zeus waiting to be tackled by an unexpected wave.

For example, one way to overdo it would be to assign too many tasks for the students to do during a reading schedule. This is true for the amount of work you give yourself as well.

In the scenario shared throughout this text, the teacher started her journey by creating a literacy-group binder using a book, *Fifty Reproducible Strategy Sheets That Build Comprehension during Independent Reading (Grades 4–8)*, by Anina Robb (2003); and a website, Literature Circles (www.edselect.com/literature_circles.htm), created by Pat Elliott. Although they are both resources, you can easily incorporate too much.

Another example of allowing overzealous feelings to get the best of you, like they did for the teacher in the scenario, is if you create too much for the use of a literacy group. For example, the binder that was created had different sections in it for each of the reading processes (before, during, and after).

The first section could hold before-reading graphic organizers, the second section could hold during-reading graphic organizers, the third section could have literacy-role graphic organizers, the fourth section could have after-reading graphic organizers, and the last section could have after-reading final projects (see chapter 5 for more on after-reading assessments).

To avoid some potential problems with the use of materials, you should avoid having the students copy one graphic organizer from each section into their literacy-response journals, which would take a day or two, depending on the class. Also avoid having them vote in groups for the book they want to read based on the introductions you provide for them. Here is where you want to pay the most attention, so you can avoid possible pitfalls!

Although a binder with before, during, and after strategies is a great resource, you should use it sparingly. Through the examples, you now understand how easily you can become overzealous or like a Zeus waiting to dig yourself into a deep hole!

However, do not get discouraged if your first way of organizing literacy groups does not pan out! You will self-reflect and come to know what you are doing wrong. Even if you are not sure how to fix it right away, that is okay!

LITERACY GROUPS BY THE NOVICE TEACHER

A first-year secondary school teacher had enthusiasm running through her as she took on the use of literacy groups. First of all, having the students copy graphic organizers and directions was wasting valuable learning time.

Second, she assumed students knew how to do the roles just because they copied the directions, so she did not model and they did not practice before she expected them to assume their roles. In addition, since groups voted on books, some students in the group did not get to read what they wanted, nor did students get books tailored to their reading levels and abilities.

Finally, with all the copying, not much class discussion and reading were occurring. By the end of the first literacy group, the students were frustrated and so was the teacher!

This overzealous teacher spent the first two weeks of school acclimating the students to classroom procedures and expectations and teaching the students strategies they could use to help themselves get unstuck when meaning breaks down, such as highlighting for purpose and attacking unfamiliar words using context clues. However, she did not teach them any strategies related to their roles for literacy groups.

The novice teacher knows she needs to stop and rewind. She has a mess that she needs to go back and clean up before it gets bigger and it becomes permanently stuck in the minds of the students that literacy groups are too hard to be a part of and no fun. Therefore, this chapter reveals how to successfully establish the proper amount of student and teacher accountability with literacy groups.

DISCUSSION DIRECTOR

When you are little, you are full of questions. Everything is a mystery to you; you make your parents exhausted trying to solve that mystery.

With every question that you ask, you build a new understanding, and with that new understanding come additional questions and inquiry. It is the belief of this book that teachers have the opportunity to foster the inquisitiveness that kids have, so that as they walk through the classroom doors and become students, learning becomes a lifelong mystery!

And so this new and overzealous teacher described in the scenario gathers twenty-four copies of the local newspaper, about five textbooks, a few poems, a few quality picture books, and some short stories and nonfiction articles to use with modeling strategies. She is back to the drawing board.

The teacher displays a text on the overhead projector and reads it aloud to the class. She reads the piece through one time, and then she goes back and starts posing questions that require answers to be formed using prior knowledge (schema) and new information that the author has provided. She records her questions in the margins of the text.

Once she finishes reading the text a second time and recording her questions, the teacher explains to the students the importance of asking questions beyond the text and the importance of recording the questions in the margins. You should do both, to validate and guide your thinking as you continue to read the text.

For example, if you modeled asking questions using a text called "What's a Yankee Doodle?" reprinted in Week-by-Week Homework for Building Reading Comprehension and Fluency, by Mary Rose

(2002, p. 20), then you might have a few questions that come to mind, such as the following: Why are Americans viewed so poorly? How did the British soldiers feel about Americans' reactions? Why did the American soldiers sing the song?

This is when the novice teacher realizes the importance of thinking aloud, so students can see how a good reader interacts with text. This is an extremely important thing for content-area teachers to do for their students because reading to learn from a textbook is different from simply listening to a teacher or reading a novel.

Vacca and Vacca (2005) explain this practice further as an opportunity for the teacher to share out loud with the class his or her inner thoughts while reading the text.

Accordingly, students will better understand the strategies the teacher uses during the modeling, because it provides a solid visual example of how the mind should actively act in response to reading, demonstrating for students how to get unstuck and rebuild meaning from the text.

Although this teacher is new to secondary education, she has some experience at the elementary level, so she uses a lot of quality picture books for this purpose.

In addition, she always reads a text twice and sometimes three times, because each time she realizes something new or notices different information, just like when you watch a movie more than once and notice details on the second viewing that you did not catch the first time.

Every time you reread, you have a new agenda; thus, you pay closer attention to different parts or words. If a text is longer, such as a textbook chapter or a novel, you should just reread parts of the whole text to obtain new meanings that you missed on the first read.

You can even tag a section, using a sticky note with an "RR" on it, to indicate that you need to go back and look at that page again. You can also tag a page with a question mark, to indicate a need for clarification, or an exclamation point, to indicate importance.

You should wait until the second read to think of questions and record them, so your mind can have time to pull from your schema and categorize or file the new information coming in from the text, in order to form further thought-provoking questions pertaining to the text. These questions should require you to reach beyond the text to arrive at answers or draw conclusions (also known as *making inferences*).

The exception to the rule here is that you may also record questions during your first read to help enhance understanding of the text. In this scenario, the teacher also explains how inferences help form questions that expand the reader's understanding of text and form new opinions. Thus, questions and inferences are like reading and writing: they go hand in hand.

The teacher records the questions to validate her thoughts and to allow her mind to continue thinking without getting caught up in one question. Thus, her mind can act like a river and continue to flow with thought-provoking questions.

In addition, recording the questions allows her to return to them after the reread to formulate answers to the questions. This usually leads to further inquiry, but ultimately it enhances understanding of the information presented in the text.

Once the teacher finishes explaining and modeling the process for the students on day 1, she puts another text on the overhead projector for the class to begin practicing with whole-class support and teacher guidance on day 2.

During this scaffolding process, she has one student read the entire text aloud to the class. Then she has a different student reread the text aloud to the class, stopping after each paragraph for classmates to share questions, which she records in the margins for them. They usually start with literal questions; but, with practice and guidance, they get better at asking interpretive and analytical questions.

The teacher discovers that this day is also a wonderful opportunity to talk about *question-answer relationship* (QAR). This is a strategy that teaches students what types of questions are being asked and where the answers to those questions can be found. There are three types of questions: literal, interpretive, and analytical.

Literal questions (also known as *direct-text questions*) are questions to which the answers can be found in the text.

Interpretive questions (also known as *author-and-you questions*) are questions that require the students to use the text and their repertoire of knowledge to draw conclusions and make inferences about the text.

Analytical questions (also known as *on-your-own questions*) are the highest level of questions. They require the student to search beyond the text for answers. The responses may come from another source or from personal experiences. (See appendix B for a handout on the QAR cycle.)

On day 3, the teacher provides small groups with a text for them to practice the process of asking questions, while she walks around and observes and provides assistance as needed. Once they record their questions, they label them as literal, interpretive, or analytical, for further practice on the strategy.

On day 4, the students practice with just a partner; and finally, on day 5, they read a text independently and ask and record their own questions in the margins.

Then they do a *think-pair-share*. This is a strategy where students *think* about the idea or lesson on their own while interacting with the text. After a few minutes, they each get together with a classmate (i.e., *pair* up) to discuss their thinking. This provides them with independent learning and partner learning, as well as clarification. Next, each student gets with one other person to reach a final consensus.

Finally, they *share* their conclusions with the whole class. It is a great strategy to use when students are practicing a concept, skill, or strategy, and it can be used with any subject area. Keep in mind that the practice articles can come from multiple sources, including such possibilities as the newspaper or magazines.

At last, the students feel good about asking thought-provoking questions in order to fulfill the literacy role of discussion director. Of course, if they do not seem comfortable, you will need to provide them with additional practice and time to develop the strategy.

On the other hand, if they are ready to move forward, you will want to explain that the discussion director is also responsible for keeping the group members on task and watching the time, in order to wrap up the group within a reasonable time frame.

Many students get excited about being in charge of a group of peers. However, remind them that everyone will have the opportunity to experience the discussion-director role. Of course, there may be some moans that will go along with this reminder, as it will take some students out of their comfort zone!

Figures 4.1 and 4.2 provide examples of what the discussion director can record in his or her literacy-response journal before, during, or after reading. This also allows you to ensure the students are reading the material, because they will not be able to ask higher-level questions if they are not truly reading the text. Keep in mind that it takes time to develop deep critical-thinking probes.

The students are ready to try out their new literacy role in the "real world" setting, so they choose new books/texts, and everyone is responsible for being the discussion director for a two-week period. It should be successful! The students usually do a great job bringing thought-provoking questions to class each day, and they really get into answering them, too.

Although you still may not have all students reading the books they want within their reading levels, just take a deep breath and remind yourself, "I can only fix one thing at a time!"

Figure 4.1. Sample Discussion-Director Literacy Role

Discussion Director

4/28   Why do you think Despereaux didn't want to eat the book?

A: he likes reading

4/29   What was the beat to call the mouse council?

A: boom, boom, tat-tat

4/30   Who loves Despereaux, and who does he love back?

A: Princess Pea

5/1   What was Despereaux doing when Furlough came to get him?

A: reading

5/2   What is the rat's name?

A: Roscuro

5/3   What were they going to eat?

A: cake

5/4   So far, how do you like the book?

(opinion)

5/5   Who's your favorite character? Why?

(opinion)

5/6   What was the king doing when Despereaux found him in Pea's room, and why was he doing it?

A: crying (infer)

Source: From Erica Myers, a secondary student (2008). Reprinted by permission of the student's guardian.

Figure 4.2. Sample Discussion-Director Literacy Role

Discussion Director

2/4/08
1. Do you think that Harriet is a good person? Why?
2. Did you think when Harriet was helping the mother cow that it was interesting?
3. Did last night's reading interest you? Why?

2/5/08
1. Do you think Harriet gets the recognition she deserves? Why?
2. What would you do with Harriet's beat-up car if you were her? Support.
3. Is Harriet a good vet? How do you know?

2/6/08
1. Where do you think Harriet is from?
2. Do you think it would be embarrassing to be sent a letter telling you to attend a dance?

Source: From a secondary student (2008). Reprinted by permission of the student's guardian.

THOUGHTFUL CONNECTOR

Life is about experiencing new things. Each day that you wake up and live, you are creating lifelong experiences that get permanently stored into your schema.

As a child, your experiences are limited, but as you age and as you explore through living and reading, you gain necessary experiences that are crucial to learning. You see, your experiences that are stored in your schema are referred to in school as *prior knowledge*, and it is that prior knowledge that allows you to learn new material in a meaningful way, through connections.

When your mind is able to connect a past experience with something new, you are learning. Then your brain transfers the new information from short-term to long-term memory and stores that new piece of information in your schema, next to your connected experience. The brain expands your repertoire of knowledge and experiences.

The following week in the scenario, the teacher uses the same process to teach making connections. She models the strategy first with a picture book, *Grandpa's Face*, by Eloise Greenfield (1988), while thinking aloud. Next, she explains that making connections is another excellent during-reading strategy that students use to relate to the text in different ways and enhance the meaning of the text.

There are three types of connections that one makes: text-to-self, text-to-text, and text-to-world connections. It is best to allow students to learn and practice each one separately.

In this scenario, the teacher starts with text-to-self connections because it is the easiest for students to master. She opens the picture book chosen for the think-aloud and begins reading it to the students. Of course, you may choose to use any form of text to introduce this strategy.

Once she has read something that sparks a personal memory, she stops and thinks aloud, "I love my papa like Tamika loves her grandpa, and I am very close to my nanny and papa because they helped raise me when I was a little girl."

The teacher continues to read, and she explains to the students that they do not have to make a connection for each page. The connection should be natural and personal.

"I used to walk with my nanny after school up to the grocery store, just to get away and have someone to talk to about my day or how things were going at home," the teacher shares openly with her students as a text-to-self connection. Usually, once the students catch on, their hands pop up and stories are shared about their experiences with their grandparents.

The next day, the teacher uses a text on the overhead projector to continue modeling text-to-self connections for the students. As she reads the text, she shares any text-to-self connections she has with the class, and marks that part of the text with "TS" to remind herself where the connection is made. By marking the text, you can easily refer back to it during group discussion.

Oftentimes a student adds in his or her own text-to-self connection, such as, "I was playing with matches outside when the fire touched my finger, so I dropped the entire book of matches and caught a few leaves on fire out back. I started yelling and my mom came outside. She was so mad at me, but she put the fire out anyway," the student shares in response to "The Triangle Shirtwaist Fire" from *Read-Aloud Anthology*, by Janet Allen and Patricia Daley (2004, p. 19).

"Very good. That was a great example of a text-to-self connection," the teacher confirms enthusiastically.

The next week, the teacher models, and they practice text-to-text connections the first two days with two different forms of texts. She explains to them that this is where a text that you are reading reminds you of another text you read in the past. The teacher uses the same picture book and overhead transparency text for familiarity. The teacher also records the text-to-text connections in the margins with a "TT."

For the remainder of the week, the students follow the same scaffolding process that supports the gradual release method the teacher used for asking questions. This teaching method is successful because you are giving students more control of their learning with each day they walk through the classroom door, which goes well with the idea of having a student-centered classroom.

The "I do," "we do," "they do," and "you do" process promotes the students to eventually do 75 percent of the teaching and learning from each other, which increases their ability to retain new information.

Last but not least, the following week the teacher models, and they practice, text-to-world connections. This is usually the most difficult one for students to master due to their limited experience and knowledge of the world they live in. The teacher explains to the class that this is when the text you are reading reminds you of something learned from television shows, magazines, movies, or newspapers.

Again, for familiarity and comfort, the teacher uses the same picture book and overhead-transparency text from the first two days. Imagine how helpful this text repetition is for content learning. As with the other connections, she records the text-to-world connections in the margins of the text, noting them with a "TW."

By the end of the third week, the students are more confident about making connections and fulfilling the literacy role of thoughtful connector. In addition, they are confident with the context due to multiple reads. Figure 4.3 is an example of what the thoughtful connector records in his or her literacy-response journal during reading.

Now the students have two literacy roles to choose from for literacy groups, and they are glad—because after two literacy cycles, they are ready for a new role! At this point your literacy groups consist of a discussion director and a thoughtful connector. The students are encouraged to put their own personal touch into the roles, which makes it even more meaningful and interesting.

Unfortunately, you may notice at times that the questions and connections can lack substance; but it is still a huge improvement from their first attempts at the strategies prior to modeling and practicing in the rewind process, and you should continue to hold them accountable for quality work. At other times, they can surprise you with their questions and connections. As the students move up in grade level, the depth of response also improves.

Figure 4.3.   Sample Thoughtful-Connector Literacy Role

Connector

4/28/08
I can connect to Despereaux because I know what it's like to be different from everyone else sometimes.

4/29/08
I can connect to Pea because I like rats but my mom won't let me have one because she thinks they are nasty.
I can connect to Despereaux because I know what it's like to do something you are not supposed to.

4/30/08
I can connect to Despereaux because I know what it's like to get into trouble.
I can also connect to him because I also would rather be in light than the dark.

5/1/08
I can connect to Despereaux because I know what it's like to talk to a very strange person.
I can connect to Chiaroscuro because I know what it's like to not know what you want from life.

Source: From a secondary student (2008). Reprinted by permission of the student's guardian.

For example, Gabrielle writes, "I can connect to Despereaux because I know what it's like to be different from everyone else sometimes." Although she does not record more on this text-to-self connection, she does elaborate on it within the group during her sharing opportunity, which surprises the teacher in this scenario due to the personal level of the connection.

ARTFUL ARTIST

As a child, you love to explore with different mediums to create images anywhere and everywhere you can. You draw on table surfaces, walls, and on paper. Your parents' refrigerator is full of pictures you drew from images your mind's eye pictured.

It is the teacher's opportunity to nurture that desire to create what the mind imagines and teach students to focus their ability to draw with textual support. The reading strategy presented in this section does just that for students who love to draw.

It is week 8 in the process in this scenario, and the teacher finally feels like learning is taking place within literacy groups in a productive and successful manner.

The next literacy role she works on with the class is that of the artful artist, which relates to the strategy known as *visualizing*!

Visualizing is a strategy good readers will use during reading to maintain comprehension. Their minds create "still shots" or "motion pictures" of the text based on prior knowledge and the words the author uses to describe the scene. The teacher uses another picture book to model this strategy, but she does not show the students the pictures and instead describes aloud what she pictures in her mind's eye as she reads out loud.

For this example, the teacher introduces visualizing and illustrating the same way as the other strategies. She begins by reading a picture book, *Owl Moon*, by Jane Yolen (1987). Remember, you may choose any text you want to model a strategy. She chooses this book for its descriptive language.

While she reads, she stops to share what she sees in her mind's eye several times. "The author's words allow me to see stone statues of trees that reach to the sky, creating massive shadows down below," the teacher shares with the students after reading the first page.

She resumes reading the book aloud and stops to share another image. "That part of the text made me think of a pitch-black area where I can barely see anything around me, like I have my eyes closed."

She continues this reading and sharing through the rest of the story. Then she reads the picture book a second time, showing the illustrations to the class and discussing what she described from her mind's eye and what the author has illustrated to support the text.

On day 2, the teacher gives each student a copy of a text and places a transparency copy on the overhead. The visual on the overhead is a graphic organizer with four empty boxes. They read the text together and stop after each paragraph to discuss what they see in their minds' eyes.

Then the teacher illustrates one description in each box on the overhead projector. For this demonstration and practice, she uses a poem, "There's a Cobra in the Bathroom," by Kalli Dako (found in *Read-Aloud Anthology* by Janet Allen and Patrick Daley; 2004, p. 18). After the first stanza, the students are asked to stop following along and draw a picture in the first box of what they see in their minds' eyes.

By the time they finish the poem, they have four excellent illustrations to support the meaning of the poem. The class then discusses the purpose of the poem and why the teacher did not believe the little girl about the snake in the bathroom. (See appendix C for the visualizing handout used on the overhead projector.)

Oftentimes, students really enjoy this strategy, and they usually laugh and do not mind working with this poem and the illustrating process.

For the rest of the week, the students follow a group practice and a partner practice for visualizing. They use a newspaper article for a group practice and a magazine article for the partner practice. It is important for the students to try the strategy with many forms of text. The bottom line is that they love to draw because it does not feel like "school."

On the last day of practice, allow a museum walk around the class to enjoy the different images illustrated by the students based on what they saw in their minds' eyes.

A museum walk can be done for any type of work. You can either hang the work or lay it out on the desks, and students can walk around the classroom to observe and discuss different perspectives on the lesson. It is enjoyable to hear them discussing the differences and similarities among their drawings as they walk around the classroom.

"I saw the boy floating under the hot sun in the middle of the ocean too, but my boy looks different than your boy," one student notes to her classmate.

On the last day of this strategy, the students cheer. The teacher cannot help but inquire as to why. "Are you that excited to leave my class for the weekend?" she asks.

"NO! When we come back on Monday, we will have another literacy role to choose from," one student says with a huge smile across her face. No doubt, the students will take the artful-artist role and make it wonderful. You will recognize the amount of talent running through your classes, and it will be amazing!

Figures 4.4 and 4.5 are excellent examples, from two different students' literacy-response journals, of entries produced as artful artist.

Notice that these examples are designed in comic-strip format; however, your students can choose to depict their scenes from the text any way they wish to, for example with one drawing per page or two drawings per page. The design layout is not as important as the actual product produced by the students based on the most important information represented in the text by the author.

This is usually their favorite role; it is certainly a wonderful product of learning to look over when journals are collected for grading! Of

Figure 4.4.   Sample Artful-Artist Literacy Role
Source: From a secondary student (2007). Reprinted by permission of the student's guardian.

Figure 4.5.   Sample Artful-Artist Literacy Role
Source: From Liberty Sales, a secondary student (2008). Reprinted by permission of the student's guardian.

course, most people enjoy drawing even if they are not great at it. For this reason, you should enjoy teaching this strategy and looking at the students' drawings.

CHARACTER CAPTAIN

Every person has a story to tell. You can stop and record key events that take place or write down comments that are made in a personal diary or journal. It is very natural to live life and create a story, but it is difficult to stop and acknowledge those events or comments or even draw conclusions and learn from them. This is why students generally have a difficult time with the role of character captain.

Remember, they have to be taught how to slow down and review, record, and analyze the character(s). However, it is an important skill to master, so that is why the character captain is the fourth literacy role. Let the challenge begin!

At the start of the tenth week of this process, the teacher in the scenario shows how to complete a character analysis in order to fulfill the literacy role of character captain. Now, mind you, the students are still doing literacy groups during the process of learning the new roles, so they have a lot on their plates. Of course, the teacher starts by reading a picture book aloud to the class.

For this strategy, she chooses to read *Gregory Cool*, by Caroline Binch (1994), because there is really only one main character throughout the story—so it is an easy way to learn how to follow a character through a text, record observations, and code those observations with categories (also defined as *analysis*).

She starts modeling by simply reading the picture book aloud to the class. She reads this entire book about a boy who visits his grandparents in a different part of the world and realizes they do not have all the luxuries he has with his parents. The teacher reads with feeling and expression.

Then the teacher explains to the students,

> Today we are going to start understanding a new literacy role, character captain. The role of character captain represents the reader's ability to analyze the main character throughout the story. In order to analyze a character, you must create separate parts or elements or categories for the character. For this purpose, you will look for just a few parts:
>
> 1. What does the character say?
> 2. What does the character do?
> 3. How does the character feel?
> 4. What do other characters in the story say or think about the character?

Afterward the teacher draws a character-analysis web on the white board so that the visual learners will grasp what she has just explained. "Now, I'm going to read the book a second time, and we will fill in the character-analysis web together," she explains to the class.

"In order to fill in the web, we are going to have to use some of our inference skills, so who can remember what it means to make an inference?" she asks the class. (See appendix D for a blank character-analysis web.)

"That is where we use what the author tells us and what we already know to make a conclusion," Zsuzie answers with certainty.

"You got it, Zsuzie. We are going to need to read between the lines to draw conclusions on the subject of Gregory's feelings and thoughts about his situation, as well as how his family feels regarding his behaviors," the teacher reiterates.

When they finish the second reading and fill in the character-analysis web on the white board, the students will learn that it is easier than they think.

"Oh, but we are not done with the responsibilities of the character captain just yet," the teacher interjects.

"We now need to complete the second half of the character captain's set of responsibilities, which involves discussing the data collected during reading," she informs the class.

"Take a few minutes to go back over the web on the white board. Ask yourself, 'Are there any patterns of behavior?' 'What do those patterns reveal to me?' and 'What do the patterns say about the character?'" Thus she leads the class to discuss the data collected. Figure 4.6 provides a visual example of the character-analysis web that the class has generated during the second reading of the book.

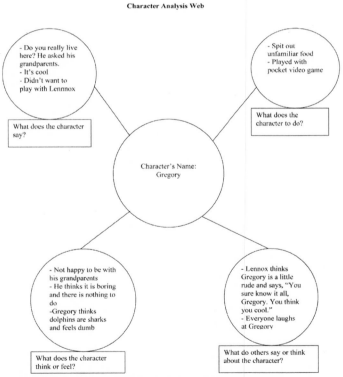

Character Analysis Web

- Do you really live here? He asked his grandparents.
- It's cool
- Didn't want to play with Lennnox

What does the character say?

- Spit out unfamiliar food
- Played with pocket video game

What does the character to do?

Character's Name: Gregory

- Not happy to be with his grandparents
- He thinks it is boring and there is nothing to do
- Gregory thinks dolphins are sharks and feels dumb

What does the character think or feel?

- Lennox thinks Gregory is a little rude and says, "You sure know it all, Gregory. You think you cool."
- Everyone laughs at Gregory

What do others say or think about the character?

Figure 4.6. Character-Analysis Web Created for Caroline Binch's _Gregory Cool_ (1994)

After a few minutes, the teacher asks for thoughts, "All right, class, what did you notice?"

"Gregory went into the vacation with a negative attitude," Samantha shares.

"It made it hard for his cousin to like him because Gregory was so negative about everything," Devin explains.

"It wasn't until he met those two men and saw things differently that he stopped being negative and started having a better time with his cousin and grandparents," Chris states.

"Very good, class, this is the type of discussion that should come about from the character-captain role. You may follow more than one character, but be sure all the characters you choose to analyze are important to the story. In other words, you will see them throughout the entire text and they are each a part of the main idea," she explains to the class.

"Also, I would like for you to draw a profile or just the head of the character you have chosen to follow. Nice start today! We will continue practicing character analysis tomorrow and the rest of the week. Have a good day," the teacher concludes.

For this scenario, the teacher follows the same gradual release pattern for character captain. On day 2, she puts a character-analysis web on the overhead projector and passes out a one-page text. She has the students read it together, then reread the text silently in their heads. Next, they work together to fill in the character-analysis web and discuss the patterns.

The following day, she gives the students a newspaper article highlighting a basketball player. They read this article in small groups and complete a character-analysis web. Finally, they discuss their findings and patterns with the whole class.

Then they do a partner reading with a short story from their textbook and complete a character-analysis web with their partners, following it up with a think-pair-share to confirm conclusions. By the end of the week, they will have it down! "We are ready to use character captain in literacy groups," a student demands on the fifth day.

"I agree, you all are ready." The teacher smiles as she speaks.

Thus, eleven weeks have come and gone in this process, and the students are no longer dreading participation in literacy groups. They are forming a strong repertoire of strategies to use with multiple forms of text, and building confidence to be successful readers in order to learn within their content-area classes. Figure 4.7 is a wonderful representation of the character-captain role for literacy groups.

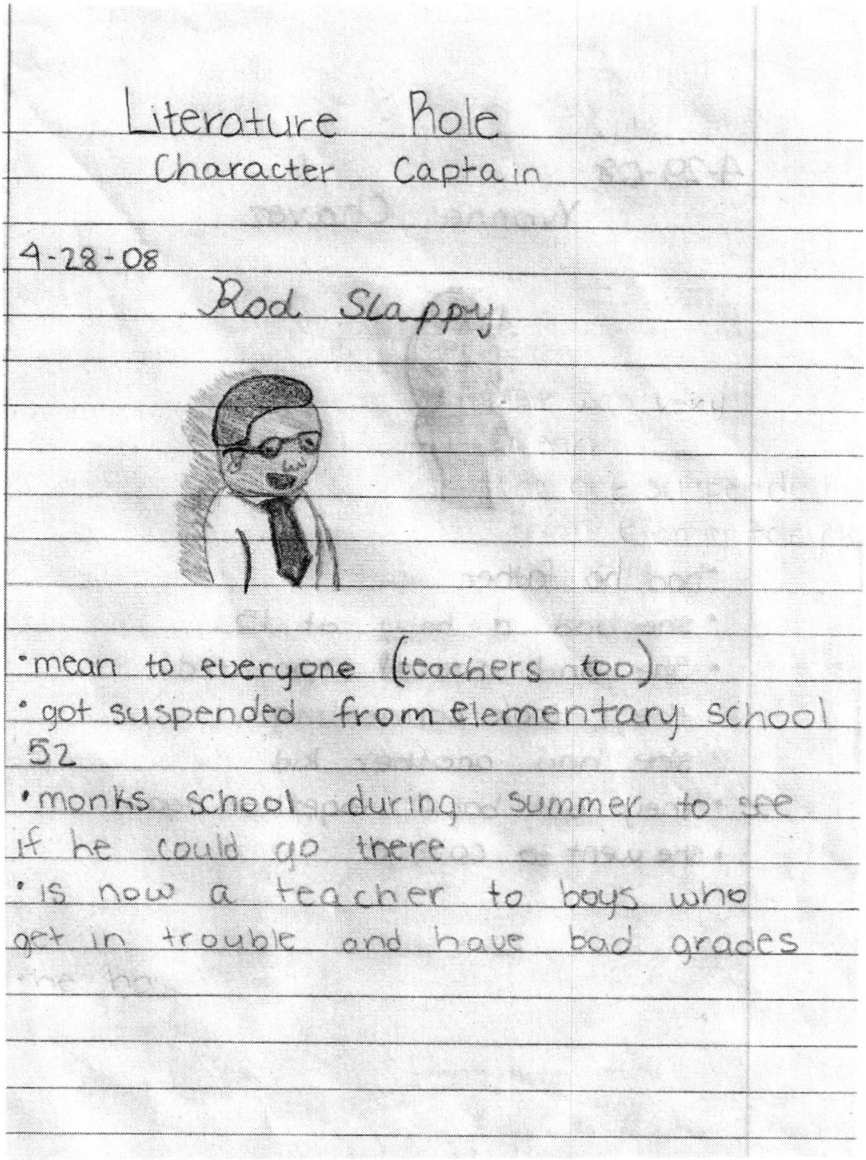
Literature Role
Character Captain

4-28-08

Rod Slappy

•mean to everyone (teachers too)
•got suspended from elementary school 52
•monks school during summer to see if he could go there
•is now a teacher to boys who get in trouble and have bad grades

Figure 4.7. Sample Character-Captain Literacy Role

Source: From Anna Gasztold, a secondary student (2008). Reprinted by permission of the student's guardian.

"What are we learning next week?" a student asks the teacher as they clean up to go home that Friday.

"Our last literacy role, literary luminary!" she replies.

LITERARY LUMINARY

Most people pick up a text and read with very little thought as to the relationship each sentence plays to the overall theme of the text. You are probably guilty of this as well at times. However, some parts of the text are so important to the understanding of the text that they should be revisited and discussed. It is for this reason that literary luminary is the fifth literacy-group role.

The literary-luminary role provides students with the ability to re-examine text and discuss its importance and connection to the overall theme of the text. This is especially useful when you are working with longer texts and a second or third read is not feasible. So jump back into the scenario and find out how to introduce and guide students with the use of this new strategy.

"Good morning. I hope everyone had a restful weekend. Today I will introduce our final literacy role, literary luminary. I have chosen a picture book that requires us to pay close attention in order to understand the author's theme, or the message of the story. I will read it once for us to just listen to and then again for discussion," the teacher explains as the class gets started.

The teacher opens the picture book, *The Talking Eggs*, by Robert D. San Souci (1989), and begins to read. The students usually hang on every word as they discover the weirdness of this book.

Once the teacher finishes the first read, she explains to the students that the literary luminary's job is to choose special parts of the text to be revisited because they are funny, interesting, confusing, important, or powerful. Through emphasizing these parts, learning transfers from short-term to long-term memory.

The literary luminary records the page number, the paragraph(s), and the sentence(s) he or she has chosen to highlight for the group discussion. You can also tag it with a sticky note (LL), in order to locate it quickly.

"Let's take another look at our story." The teacher draws a chart on the board with four columns and two rows. She labels each column with a heading: *Page Number*, *Paragraph*, *Sentence*, and *Reason*. Then she reads the picture book a second time, but this time she stops when she gets to a part she wants to highlight and discuss.

She stops at the part where the main character helps the old woman complete tasks around the house. The teacher continues to read about the girl going into the barn and taking the eggs the old woman told her to take.

At this point, the teacher stops reading and writes on the board within the chart, while also explaining what she is doing. "I am stopping to record an important part of the story, page 15, paragraph 6, sentence 3, because this is where the author truly demonstrates the good and honest character in Blanche, which I think it is important to the overall message." Then she continues to read the story.

The teacher stops again and shares her thinking as she records later parts in the text: "I am stopping here in the text to record page 25, paragraph 2, sentence 3, because I noticed the old woman told the two girls different directions. I also want to record page 25, paragraph 4, sentence 3, because this is where the author reveals the true colors of the secondary character."

The teacher finally finishes the second read and records just a few more parts she feels are important. "Now, class, we are ready to discuss the parts I have chosen to highlight. For this part, the literary luminary gets to choose someone in the group to read the part(s) he or she has highlighted out loud to the rest of the group. Then the group gets to try and guess why the literary luminary chose that part."

Finally, the literary luminary shares his or her reason for highlighting a particular part of the text, and further discussion can occur if the group feels it is necessary. For example, after the teacher shares her reasons, she may also want to discuss why the author chose to represent different characters with certain objects.

"You know that saying, 'rotten egg'? I think the author used this symbolism to represent good and evil," Steven shares with the class.

Their discussion continues for the entire class, and the students even ask the teacher to reread the part in the book where the old woman takes her head off. It is evident the book is that good! However, you will need to read the story for yourself to discover the ending of this wonderful picture book.

There are many amazing-quality picture books out there that teachers can use to introduce strategies, skills (e.g., main idea, supporting details, compare and contrast, cause and effect), and new concepts (such as the Holocaust), but you can choose to use any form of text to introduce, practice, and master strategies and skills.

The next day, the teacher passes out a text for the students to read in groups of four or five. She asks them to read it once to get a basis of the text, and then read it again to identify something funny, interesting, confusing, important, or powerful. "Pick only one thing per group to start off with," she clarifies for them.

Next, they share their highlighted parts with the whole class for discussion. On day 3, they do another small-group practice. This form of scaffolding proves successful in the learning process.

By the end of the week, she provides each student with a newspaper article. She has chosen a newspaper article because students usually have difficulty understanding that type of text; and, up to this point, students were choosing to highlight parts that were funny, interesting, or important.

In addition, she wants them to have experience recognizing confusing parts as well, since the literary luminary role is a great way to monitor comprehension and mark a part to receive clarification from group members. They each read the article one time in their heads. In this example, it does not take long for hands to shoot up all around the room. "I don't know what this article is about," Jackson honestly admits.

The article is "Bringing Students the World," by Andrew Skerritt, from the *Pasco Times* (2007). "Good! Let's look at the article for a re-read together. Jackson, why don't you read the first paragraph for us?" the teacher asks.

"'In 2004, she spent time in China as a Fullbright scholar. She spent a week in India with former President Jimmy Carter and Habitat for Humanity International building houses.' Who is she?" Jackson asks after he reads the first paragraph.

"That's a good question, Jackson. You have some choices to help yourself. You could look at the photos and captions, or you could continue to read to see if your question will be answered in the next paragraph," the teacher explains.

"I will keep reading. 'One day last week, Gates' third grade class was studying ancient cultures. With all the state testing requirements, there's less time for kids to learn social studies, so they are using the reading comprehension and writing.' Okay so she is Gates, right?" Jackson inquires.

"Oh yeah, right here in the caption: 'Kathy Gates' class.' So she is a teacher, and her name is Kathy," Jackson thinks aloud to the class.

"Excellent problem solving, Jackson. Have we read enough yet to begin to build an understanding of the text?" the teacher asks.

Notice how the teacher probes the students to allow them to discover answers on their own instead of simply telling them the answer. It does take more time, but you are establishing the learning expectations and environment you want for group instruction for the entire year—all of which support a student-centered learning atmosphere!

"No. I'll read," Jenny volunteers.

"For the past four years, Brooksville Elementary has been engaged in an experiment educators call global studies learning. Designed to get many of these students from working-class families exposed to the world beyond their small Southern hometown, global studies has had some tangible benefits. It has been credited with improving test scores. Students are exposed to the culture customs and history of other nations." Okay, I want to mark this part as a 'literary luminary' because it is confusing to me," Jenny admits.

"Okay, Jenny. Let's look at that paragraph again. What does the author mean by 'engaged in an experiment'?" the teacher asks.

"Isn't an experiment like science?" Nathan asks.

"Yes, Nathan, it is."

"I don't get it. What does that have to do with school?" Nathan asks.

"Well, here they are referring to a research experiment where people go into a school and work with the teachers and students and write down what they see. They sometimes give a test before and after learning the new way, in order to see if the new way of learning helped the students learn more or not," the teacher explains to the class.

When students cannot figure something out, it is your job to provide a way over the roadblock, which can be by asking a question, providing background knowledge, or offering an explanation.

"Oh, like we do in here with testing color?" Jenny clarifies.

"Yes, you got it!" the teacher responds.

They spend the rest of the class rereading this article and taking turns highlighting confusing parts in the text. Then they walk through the process of figuring out what the author means. By the end of the week, they have experienced literary luminary for fun and for clarification.[1]

Figure 4.8 is an example of what the literary luminary records in his or her literacy-response journal during reading, in order to bring it to the group for discussion the next day.

LITERACY GROUPS WITH A TWIST

Every day is a new day! With each new day come lessons learned and changes made. Fortunately, the teacher in this scenario experiences many wonderful opportunities to feel success, and makes it through twelve weeks of the literacy-group process. It is a wonderful feeling of

Figure 4.8.   Sample Literary-Luminary Literacy Role

<table>
<tr><td colspan="2" align="center">Literary Luminary</td></tr>
<tr><td colspan="2">1/9
page: 9; paragraph: 4; sentence: all
  I chose this paragraph to help give an image of Tyray's father.</td></tr>
<tr><td colspan="2">1/10
page: 19; paragraph: 3; sentence: all
  He's using her to get Amberlynn jealous.</td></tr>
<tr><td colspan="2">1/11
page: 27; paragraph: 3; sentence: all
  It's where he finds the gun.</td></tr>
<tr><td colspan="2">1/12
page: 34; paragraph: 4; sentence: all
  It seems that since Darrell stood up to Tyray that everyone can.</td></tr>
<tr><td colspan="2">1/13
page: 46; paragraph: 9; sentence: all
  What does it tell you about Tyray's father? He's so tough.</td></tr>
<tr><td colspan="2">1/14
page: 58; paragraph: 3; sentence: all
  I chose this paragraph because Lark is so nice but Tyray isn't nice to her.</td></tr>
</table>

Source: From Liberty Sales, a secondary student (2008). Reprinted by permission of the student's guardian.

success because you do not have to do it alone; the students help you the entire journey, and that is awesome!

The thirteenth week is the start of a new literacy-group cycle, so it is perfect timing. The students are so excited to finally have all the pieces to the puzzle available for use. In addition, you are ready to surprise them with a new twist to make literacy groups even better! See how the teacher in this scenario adds a little twist to the journey.

"Good morning class! Before we vote on books for literacy groups today, I want to revisit one more topic." Moans and groans come from all over the room.

"Wait, it's a good thing," she reassures them. "Instead of taking out one sheet of paper for each group to write your choices on, I want everyone to take out a sheet of paper and put only your name on it and number it from 1 to 5. You will choose your own book today. Let me remind you to listen carefully to the Lexile level, number of pages, and synopsis before you make a choice."

The entire class cheers and shuffles for paper. They have wanted to choose a book on their own since the beginning.

The teacher introduces each book. "Your first choice is *Sadako and the Thousand Paper Cranes*, by Eleanor Coerr. It is nonfiction, the length is 65 pages, and it has a 630 Lexile." Then she reads the summary on the back of the book. "Your next book choice is *Mick Harte was Here*, by Barbara Park. It is realistic fiction, the length is 89 pages, and it has a 730 Lexile." She continues this process for all five choices.

When the teacher is done introducing the books, the students write down what book they want as their first choice, second choice, and so on. Next, the teacher positions herself in a central location and says, "If you have *Sadako and the Thousand Paper Cranes* as your first choice, please bring me your paper."

The first five students to bring the teacher their papers get the book as their literacy-group choice for the duration of two weeks. Be sure to remind the students that there is to be no pushing and shoving. She repeats this process for each title. Then she asks for students to bring their papers for their second choice, and so on, until every student has committed to a title for literacy groups.

An alternative approach to assigning titles is to place students' names in a container, draw out names, and let each student choose a title within one hundred Lexile points of his or her score. This way it is fair and safe.

Next, the teacher assigns tables or locations in the room for the students to get together. "If you are reading *Sadako and the Thousand Paper Cranes*, sit at table 1; *Mick Harte was Here*, sit at table 2; *Tears of a Tiger*, sit at table 3; *Listening for Lions*, sit at table 4; and *Fever 1793*, sit at table 5."

After the transition, she passes out the books and the reading schedules. The reading schedule is a timetable that is created for each book to keep students organized and on task. You simply take the total number of pages and divide it by eleven days (or however many days you intend to set aside for reading), which allows you to determine what pages need to be read each day or night.

One student from each group gets to keep the schedule that the teacher writes out by gluing it onto the reading-schedule page, and everyone else copies it into their literacy-response journals. This usually takes five minutes or less, depending on the age of the students.

The reading-schedule page is the first page the students set up in order to start a new literacy-group cycle. (See appendix E for a black-line master of the reading schedule.) Table 4.1 provides you with a visual example of the type of reading schedule that the teacher creates and provides to each group at the start of the literacy cycle.

Table 4.1.   Sample Reading Schedule Given by Teacher to Students

Reading Schedule	
Book Title: Fever 1793	
Date	Pages
11/19/07	1–23
11/20/07	24–45
11/21/07	46–67
11/22/07	68–88
11/23/07	89–111
11/24/07	112–132
11/25/07	133–152
11/26/07	153–177
11/27/07	178–199
11/28/07	200–221
11/29/07	222–243

The students' literacy-response-journal page should be set up exactly like, or similarly to, the teacher-created one, in order to establish consistency.

Subsequently, the students set up the second page (the literacy role) for the literacy-group cycle in the literacy-response journal (which is a composition notebook). The student simply writes the heading *Literacy Role* at the top of the page, and underneath he or she writes what role is desired for the two-week duration. They can repeat roles, as long as no one else in the group wants the role they wish to do again. This usually takes five minutes or less, also depending on the age of the students.

If two or more students all want the same role, they have to rock-paper-scissor to make the final decision—because you always want student-centered groups, and therefore you need to encourage them to work out their differences.

They are required to fulfill their roles for each scheduled reading. Figure 4.9 is an example of what a literacy-role page looks like when filled in with work.

Finally, when they first get their books, they start by reading the title, reading the synopsis on the back, and making predictions. Then they read out loud together, using the word *popcorn* to change readers, which encourages all students to follow along. Of course, you can have them jump into groups a different way; it is up to you.

Now you have seen how to build quality literacy groups. You are ready to see how the groups run smoothly. In this scenario, the teacher

Figure 4.9.   Sample Literacy-Role Page in Literacy-Response Journal

---

Literature Role: Predictor

11/5 I think that this book is going to be about racism based on the summary on the back of the book.

11/6 I think that one of the Logan's kids will go to the Wallace Store.

11/7 I think Jeremy will tell someone who made the hole and the Logan's aren't going to get burned but threatened since they didn't speak to Jeremy.

11/8 I think Mama Logan will open up a store and give people credit when they do not have any money. Mama Logan's store is only for black people.

11/9 I think Lillian Jean is going to get threatened by Jeremy for being so mean to the Logan's.

11/10 I think that Hammer is going to move close to his family to protect them. In the end he will be the hero because he stopped racism.

Source: From Erica Myers, a secondary student (2007). Reprinted by permission of the student's guardian.

is ready to release her students to work for the first time, with all the roles working together like in chapter 1. It is truly an exciting time!

After the first day mentioned above, the teacher begins to set objectives for them while they work in groups for thirty minutes. For day 2, they are to share their roles, summarize key events to clear up any confusion that may occur after one day of reading, and read together out loud to improve oral fluency.

The following day, they discuss their likes and dislikes about the book, share their roles, and read out loud together. The last day of the week, they read independently for twenty minutes during silent independent reading (SIR) time. This is also when you come back together as a whole class to share and discuss themes across literacy groups. How are the books similar and different?

The second week with the book, they read for twenty minutes during SIR time on Monday and Friday, so you can work with students one-on-one or in small groups. You only spend about five minutes per student, and between week 1's Friday and week 2's Monday and Friday, you should be able to meet with twelve students, to help with anything they need help with understanding the text or class lessons.

During the second week, on Tuesday, they challenge the author ("why did the author have the character do . . . ?"), as well as sharing their roles and reading out loud together. Finally, the last literacy-group day of week 2, they discuss "what if?" situations, share their roles, and read out loud together. The system works very well now, and by the sixth literacy-group-cycle attempt it is safe to say this is long overdue.

THE TEACHER'S ROLE

The best thing about learning groups or literacy groups is that every person in the classroom has a role or responsibility to fulfill in order for the entire class to get the most out of the scheduled time. The teacher's job is to facilitate the process.

There are many approaches a teacher can take to use student-centered learning. One is the passive approach, in which the teacher gives the minilesson and directions and releases the students into their collaborative groups while he or she sits behind the desk checking e-mails, grading papers, or reading a book.

However, the method described in the preceding paragraph is certainly not to be recommended as an approach, if students are to reach their full potential. This approach eventually allows the students to think this scheduled learning time is not important, and they do not give it their all. Students perceive their classes as teachers portray them, so "do as I say and not as I do" is not a reasonable approach to teaching.

The other approach is the one this book is all about. In this approach, the teacher participates, guides, and observes during the entire scheduled collaborative learning time. This is the teacher's role and the teacher's responsibility to the class as a whole. Take a look at each guideline to ensure you understand how to fulfill this important part of using literacy groups.

A teacher needs to hold students accountable for their roles and participation within the collaborative groups. Therefore, part of the teacher's role is to **observe** the students regularly.

For this example, the teacher starts off by walking around the classroom and touching base with each student for at least ten seconds once she has released them into groups.

The time allows the teacher to see if the students have completed their roles in their journals; to learn about any confusion that may have occurred the night before; and to see how they are enjoying the book. The students like it because they know the teacher is holding them accountable for their roles and participation, which provides them with the classroom structure students need and desire.

The next task on the teacher's agenda is to guide the student groups who are having a difficult time digging deeper into the meaning of the text, as we saw in chapter 1. This is where the teacher walks around the room, listens to group conversation, and then chooses a group that appears to be only talking about surface meaning, so she can **guide** them to deeper thinking.

Surface meaning is recalling facts, and the teacher wants them to dig deeper—to question why the author used certain words or made a character act in a particular way, or to conclude how their text is related to the overall theme. The teacher wants them to be active learners. That means arguing with the text, questioning the text, and challenging the author.

Therefore, the teacher can guide the groups to reach this deeper thinking by simply posing questions, such as "Why do you think the author . . . ?" or "What did the author mean by . . . ?"

Many teachers want their students to see the author's intended feelings and find a way to connect the story to their lives today. This is difficult for students to do on their own, so they need the teacher to guide them to be active readers to learn new material.

Finally, the teacher's role also includes sitting down with a different group each day to **participate** in the discussion as an active group member.

The teacher needs to try to work with groups that are struggling with meaning first, and work her way around to the other groups later on in the reading schedule. This way her struggling readers or groups with more difficult text receive the teacher's help early on, to prevent meaning from breaking down and the entire book from being ruined for them.

When the teacher participates with a group, he or she should do everything the students are required to do. The teacher should share a role, which can simply mean asking questions about completed roles or providing deeper meaning from the text. Also participate in addressing the goal for the day (e.g., summarizing, "what if?", dislikes/likes). The students really enjoy this one-on-one attention from the teacher.

Then the teacher takes turns reading out loud with the group. This is good for two reasons: it allows the teacher to listen to students' oral reading, which is a skill they should be working on improving; and it allows students to hear a fluent reader as a model for their own growth.

Fluent readers usually portray tone and voice, as well as flow, when they read out loud; so the teacher should model accuracy, speed, and expression with his or her students. In addition, they think it is awesome and oftentimes will try it when it is their turn, because the teacher has established a safe zone for them to give it a try.

The bottom line is that the road you choose to go down is ultimately up to you. You may even choose something in between the two approaches; but keep in mind that the more effort you put in, the more effort your students will put into the entire learning process in your class.

The important point is to pick an approach and stick with it the entire time; consistency is extremely important with students, but you probably already know that! Good luck!

WHAT YOU HAVE LEARNED FOR PROMOTING INDEPENDENCE AND FLEXIBILITY

"Really, I love literacy groups. It gives students some time off from straight class work. It also gives us a variety of different books, so really we're still learning whether it be new vocabulary words or about an important event or person from history. I really enjoy literacy groups!" Tracie expresses on a survey given at the end of the school year.

Well, you can say the journey has finally reached its peak and you are halfway to your destination of becoming proficient readers and learners through student-centered collaboration around multiple forms of text.

It is the use of collaboration that helps students improve at reading to learn in your class, so it is significant when you implement meaningful collaboration opportunities for your students during class time (Gallagher, 2004).

In this chapter, you learned some key ideas about how to establish learning groups in your classroom. The example throughout the chapter provided many visuals to guide you; but remember from the beginning, reading about it and trying it yourself are two different matters.

Plus, every secondary-school schedule is different. For instance, at the school the teacher in this scenario works at, they are on blocked scheduling. This means she only sees her classes four times a week out of the five days.

On Monday and Friday, she sees all of her classes for fifty minutes; and she sees each of her classes two days out of the remaining three, for eighty minutes each.

Block scheduling is nice because of the variety, and the students think so too. Furthermore, the eighty-minute classes lend themselves nicely to student-centered learning; however, this method has been tested and proved to work with fifty-minute classes as well. You must use each minute in the most productive way possible.

The next chapter provides you with some wonderful ways to assess students' understanding of the books they read without testing them with a regular paper-and-pencil test. So take a bathroom break, fill up your cup, and don't forget to stretch—because it's about to get creative with after-reading assessment. Let the journey continue!

NOTE

1. Andrew Skerritt, "Bringing Students the World," *St. Petersburg Times*, St. Petersburg, Florida. Copyright 2007 by *St. Petersburg Times*. Reprinted with permission of the publisher, S. Palmer.

⑤

Differentiated Assessment

"I think literacy groups are a good way for students to get to know the people in their class better. I like them a lot better than filling in a book log or a worksheet. I also love seeing what other people have done. It's a good way to have a better understanding about the book you are reading. I enjoy it when the teacher comes and listens to the discussion and asks us questions. I enjoy doing the after-reading projects, but I would like it if there were even more to choose from in the binder. Overall, I enjoy participating in literacy groups," Chelsea shares.

WHY ASSESSMENT?

To assess or not to assess, that is the question! Many times during your life, you will be assessed or evaluated to demonstrate performance, competency, or understanding.

For example, before you can get your driver's license, you must study a manual full of rules and guidelines and then take a computer test to demonstrate your ability to recall important rules and guidelines for driving. Your hard work earns you a learner's permit, with which you can drive during the day with a licensed driver over the age of eighteen.

Oh, but you are not done being assessed just yet! You have to practice, practice, and practice driving a vehicle. Some people even take a driver-education class to further assist in the learning process of driving.

Finally, after many months of practice, you get into a vehicle with a stranger who sits in the passenger's seat with a clipboard, judging and evaluating your every move and decision. It is extremely nerve-racking, yet people put themselves through it because the end result provides them with an indescribable freedom!

Driving is not the only time where assessment occurs in your life beyond school. What about a job? Typically, your boss completes frequent evaluations in order to document your ability to do the job (and, hopefully, justify your receiving a raise). Unfortunately, assessment is a regular part of life, so why should it be any different in school?

Although tests are stressful and sometimes scary, they must be administered in order to obtain valuable information.

As a teacher, you understand the purpose of assessment. It is used as a way to monitor students' understanding of new material or comprehension of text. Assessment is used to guide students' learning, so that they know when a skill needs to be retaught or a book needs to be reread. That is exactly the reason this chapter describes the evaluation process as part of the literacy-group experience.

Since you are only able to work with twelve students individually per literacy-group cycle, and with four out of five groups per literacy-group cycle, it is extremely important that you use the literacy-response journals and the after-reading assessment as a way to monitor students' understanding of text and hold them accountable for learning your curriculum.

Of course there is no one way to do this, and the way presented in this text is certainly not perfect; but it worked for the teacher and students in the scenario shared in this text.

The after-reading assessment starts on the tenth day of having the book, because they are approaching the end. In the scenario shared throughout this text, they use a few minutes of class time to set up the third page of the literacy-response journal, which is headed, *After Reading*.

This page is important for beginning secondary students. It organizes information that students need to be successful, such as the due date. You have the students label the page "After Reading" so they are not confused later. Below the heading they put the due date, which is usually the following Monday (unless school is closed—then it is due the next official school day). Keep in mind that this works for any length of time that might be needed to complete the assigned text.

Finally, they peruse the after-reading section of the binder to choose an after-reading project, and they record their choice below the date. It is the only section of the entire binder that they ever use after the first cycle of overzealous chaos. If it is a difficult project, they may want to copy the directions onto this page too. Also, have them staple or tape their rubric in their journals on this page, to ensure they will not lose it.

The last step is for the students to check in with the teacher regarding their choices, in order to receive the rubric for the project/assessment and receive any clarification that they may need about the after-reading project. (See appendix F for the initial project rubrics.)

One suggestion to assist students with organization and responsibility is to have them staple the rubric to the after-reading page in their literacy-response journal. This way they will not lose it before they even get started on it.

The after-reading assessment is another opportunity for students to choose how they want to express their knowledge of the text. They have a choice of fifteen different projects or a quiz on the Reading Counts computer program. This program is purchased through Scholastic. This choice makes the fact that assessment or evaluation of learning must occur a little more tolerable.

THE PROJECT CHOICES

Everybody likes to have choices. When you go into a restaurant, they give you a number of food and drink choices to accommodate your personal taste buds. When you venture into a mall, you have many diverse stores to choose to shop at for your own personal style. America is about having freedom to choose, so why should school assessment be any different?

In this section of the chapter, you will read about fifteen different after-reading assessment choices that allow you to evaluate your students' understanding of their reading to learn from multiple forms of text.

The first choice is the **CD cover**. This allows the student to create song titles out of the major themes, events, or details from the text. You can clearly gather whether a student understands a text by simply evaluating the ten titles he or she creates for the back of the CD case. The CD-cover after-reading project idea is adapted from the Literature Circle Resource Center website (www.litcircles.org/Extension/extension.html), which was created by Katherine L. Schlick Noe (2004) of the College of Education at Seattle University.

The next after-reading project choice is the **collage**. The collage allows students to use pictures to represent the text's theme, events, or details. Then, on the back of the collage, the student describes what each picture represents and how it is connected to the overall theme of the text, or in other words, the "**so what?**"

The "so what?" concept is adapted from Chris Tovani's books *I Read It, but I Don't Get It: Comprehension Strategies for Adolescent Readers* (2000) and *Do I Really Have to Teach Reading? Content Comprehension, Grades 6–12* (2004).

"So what?" challenges the students to support their opinions with purpose and reason as well as to understand the connections between their opinions and ideas and the theme or main idea. The collage after-reading project idea is also adapted from the Literature Circle Resource Center website.

The third after-reading project option is the **character bookmark**. This is the students' favorite. You can even keep them and laminate them, in order to let students next year use them as bookmarks in the books they read and thereby encourage future students to read the same titles.

The character bookmark represents a wonderful opportunity for the students to create a useful tool that demonstrates their knowledge of the text.

The bookmark should be the size of an actual bookmark, so it can be used after the fact. On the front of the bookmark, the main character is illustrated and labeled. On the back of the bookmark, a description of the main character is given.

The description should state why the character was chosen by the student, how the character is important to the book, and how that importance is connected to the overall theme, also known as the "so what?" (Tovani, 2004). The character-bookmark after-reading project idea is adapted from the Literature Circle Resource Center website.

Theme images is another after-reading project choice. This one is difficult because students have to find a way to weave one word representing the theme of the text into a picture. The concept of "weaving" is what gives them difficulty.

When students choose this project, they require guidance from the teacher most of the way. You must be ready to give the extra assistance for this project, but do not pass up using it just because it presents a challenge. Once the students accomplish the task, they are very proud of themselves for the creativity and outcome. The theme-images after-reading project idea is also adapted from the Literature Circle Resource Center website.

The **game board** is another after-reading project choice. Students can mimic their favorite game to create a new game about the text they read. It is a wonderful way to evaluate their knowledge of the text because they have to create questions and answers for the game.

As students choose this project, you can save and store all the games they create, so that the students can actually play their games at the end of the school year or end of the quarter. They love this project a lot; they will ask, "When are we going to play the games we made?"

One reason you may want to wait until the end of the school year is to give all the classes an opportunity to read as many titles as possible, in order for more students to have knowledge about several different titles—thus increasing the proportion of students able to play the different games.

The students are asked to create a game that requires knowledge about the book to play. They must include the necessary pieces, such as directions and playing cards or dice. The game-board after-reading project idea is adapted from the Literature Circle Resource Center website.

The next after-reading project is the **commemorative stamp**. This is the easiest project to complete. It requires the students to create a stamp with the title of the text, a few words representing the theme or lesson learned, the price of the stamp for the text's time period, and a picture depicting an important image related to the theme.

Although it is a simple project, students can be very creative in order to get the most out of the experience. A few of the students choose to hand-draw their designs, and others take advantage of technology to render their designs. Either way is acceptable: not every student likes to draw, and so it is nice to have alternative options for creating the end result.

It also promotes the use of technology in this twenty-first-century world. The commemorative-stamp after-reading project idea is adapted from the Literature Circle Resource Center website.

Then there is the **map** after-reading project, which can be one of the most difficult projects to complete. It is recommended the students choose a different project each time, so they can challenge themselves with something new after each book. Thus, once they have completed the map, they do not need to choose it again.

The map is a visual of the main character's journey—physically, mentally, emotionally, or spiritually. This is a great project for social-studies classes. They must include a detailed map with pictures, guides, a legend, and landmarks. They have to title the journey, and the title should be related to the theme of the text.

Constructing the map takes time and a considerable amount of thought and planning, in order for it to be an accurate depiction of the main character's true journey. Luckily, the students do have the directions in the after-reading section of the literacy-group binder, where they will find a few examples created by other students. The map after-reading project idea is adapted as well from the Literature Circle Resource Center website.

The **setting pamphlet** is another after-reading project choice. Students fold a piece of white paper into thirds to create a pamphlet template. Then they design four to five important settings from the text, which represent the key places or events of the text. Below the drawing or illustration, they write a short description of what they drew and how it is important to the text.

After they create the setting pamphlets, they can display them in the media center on the circulation desk to encourage other students in the school to read the same books. It is amazing what word-of-mouth advertisement can do for a book's popularity. This concept works even if it is the teacher promoting the book by mouth.

The setting-pamphlet project is excellent for science and social-studies classes because it easily displays steps, process, or even outlines major events. The setting-pamphlet after-reading project idea is adapted from the Literature Circle Resource Center website.

One of the coolest after-reading project choices is the **main-idea belt**. The students really get creative with this one, and it lends itself beautifully to the science and social-studies classes.

They create six large, black circles, and six smaller, white circles to go on top of the black circles. Each circle depicts a different image related to the main idea of the text. They create a border that symbolizes the theme, and on the back they write a sentence or two about the picture and how it represents the main idea.

Finally, they attach all the circles with string, yarn, or ribbon. Really, they can attach the circles any way they want to and with any medium. The creativity is in their hands. The main-idea belt after-reading project idea is adapted from the Literature Circle Resource Center website.

The next after-reading project choice is the **accordion book**. The accordion-book after-reading project idea is also adapted from the Literature Circle Resource Center website.

Students repeatedly fold a piece of legal-size paper in alternating directions, creating a paper fan—except the folds are much wider, because the students have to illustrate and write on each panel. Each panel has an illustration that represents a major scene from the story, and a written description with a few sentences explaining the connection of the scene to the overall theme of the book, or the "so what?" (Tovani, 2004).

With all the hard work that is put into each of these projects/assessments, you will want to find a way to validate the students' effort. So, to promote reading and differentiated assessment, all of the projects can be displayed on a bulletin board, as a way of recognizing quality examples of after-reading projects. This display can be changed each cycle, and the students can be responsible for updating it each month.

This is a wonderful way to exhibit illustrations of the CD cover, the commemorative stamp, the game board, theme images, the character bookmark, the collage, and the main-idea belt. In addition, the students take a lot of pride in the display and are very picky as to which projects can go up for viewing.

When students get their projects up on one of the bulletin boards, they brag about it for days; but if they do not make it up there, it pushes them to try harder on the next after-reading project. It's an excellent incentive!

The master's-degree program in reading education at the University of South Florida in Tampa offers a class about multicultural children's literature. In this class, you explore all different types of genres and ways to express this knowledge of those different genres, such as through presentations, creating a multicultural-genre notebook, or doing a creator study. It is the creator study that stood out as an interesting project.

The creator-study assignment requires students to research an author who represents a culture that they have never read from before, choose one of his or her books to read, and create a presentation to share their findings with the class. You should try this project first.

For example, the teacher from the scenario in this text chose to research Sharon Draper, because a friend had bragged about the high level of interest Draper's books generated in her students. She had never heard of this author before, so it was perfect. She went to the bookstore and purchased the book her friend suggested, *Tears of a Tiger*. It was so good she read it in one day!

The next day, she jumped on the computer and typed in "Sharon Draper." She learned so much about this author, who used to be an English teacher. This was one of her favorite assignments, one she will never forget!

This is a wonderful assignment for secondary students, and it has been adapted to meet the needs of this situation, after-reading projects. This particular project choice is called **letter to the author**. The students love this project even more once others who had chosen it at the beginning start receiving letters and small gifts from their authors or their publishers.

Basically, the students read their literacy-group book, and then research the author of the book. They learn about the author's childhood and current life. The students discover the author's motivation for writing the book and other titles he or she has published, which usually leads to students reading additional titles.

Finally, the students write letters to their authors, describing who they are and why they are writing. Each student discusses a few important details that he or she has learned about the author, and what he or she enjoyed most about the author's book. It generally ends up being about one page, typed.

If the author is no longer living, the students can write to the publisher. This after-reading project provides students with very important research skills and synthesis skills that are required in order for them to be lifelong learners, and this is a fun way to meet those requirements!

Furthermore, the students end up with a great response from authors and publishers, which makes it all the more rewarding. The class in this scenario heard back from many well-known authors, such as Joseph Bruchac (author of *Skeleton Man*), Andrew Clements (author of *Things Not Seen*), and Sharon Draper (author of *Double Dutch*).

In the scenario mentioned throughout this book, one particular publisher went above and beyond when it came to responding to students' letters. Townsend Press sent several students wonderful letters on behalf of authors who are deceased, as well as another book written by one of the authors, for the students to read and enjoy. It is amazing!

Another after-reading project is the **picture-book version of the novel**. This is probably the most time-consuming because students have to take the key events and write about them in a story format, with illustrations to assist in the telling of the story.

The picture book has to be told in the student's own words, and the illustrations need to demonstrate effort, so stick figures are unacceptable; however, the student can use the Internet, clip art, or magazines to create an illustration if drawing is not his or her strong suit.

In the end, the student has a wonderful product that can be displayed in the media center for other students to view. The student can also donate the picture-book version of the novel to a local elementary school for the continuous promotion and utilization of the story. They love this idea and usually send it to a teacher they had at some time in their educational career!

In the twenty-first century, just placing your pictures into slots in a regular photo album is no longer desirable. Many people choose to store their memories in a creative fashion, with personalized sayings and objects to enhance the moment for a lifetime.

Remembering a great book should not be any different, and that is why the **scrapbook of the main character** after-reading project is also an option. It allows students to demonstrate their understanding of the text in a fun and creative way.

The students choose the most important character from the text and create a photo album of his or her life in sequential order. This is perfect for social-studies classes. They get to decorate the page, just like in a scrapbook photo album, which personalizes the main character's life for the students. They use bubbles to represent character talk, stickers, borders, and lettering, just to name a few items.

This project can also be displayed in the media center for other students from all around the school to enjoy, and then returned to its creator within a month's time. Unfortunately, since the picture-book version of the novel and scrapbook of the main character ideas have been used for years now, the originators are unknown.

The fourteenth project is the **book-box** after-reading project. This is adapted from *Fifty Literacy Strategies: Step by Step*, by Gail Tompkins (1998). (Even though it is referred to here as the fourteenth, the projects are not completed in any particular order. The students can choose to complete the projects in any order they want to, as long as they choose a different one each time to challenge themselves.)

This project has the student decorate the outside of a box with a lid to represent the main idea and theme of the text. Then five items that symbolize key events or ideas about the text are placed inside the box. One of those items is always the text itself.

Next they have to fill out an inventory checklist and attach it to the inside of the lid. The checklist tells the viewer what is in the box and why it is in the box. This explanation should show how the item is connected to the overall main idea or theme of the text. It is a great project for practicing "main idea and supporting details," which is an important literal-comprehension skill.

When the student is done, she has a beautiful representation of a book at a glance in a box. Their book boxes can be put on display in the media center for one month, to inspire other students from around the school to read that book.

They are such a big hit that students interact with the boxes by lifting up the lids and looking inside! There is usually not a single student who does not choose this project willingly. They love the idea and the creativity behind it!

The final after-reading project does not have a rubric because it is an actual guided outline, like a cloze passage, for students to write a **text review**.

The form guides them to make choices about their text, form opinions, and provide support, as well as rate their text (newspaper, magazine, book, etc.) on a scale of 1 to 10. This text review can go into a folder next to the classroom library for students to refer to if they are in need of reading suggestions for pleasure.

The form allows the students to practice explaining with support, using transitions, and identifying and defining story elements. The students who do not enjoy art-related projects really like completing this because it is guided and not too time-consuming. (See appendix G for the text-review form.)

When all is said and done, the projects are just suggestions. There are so many different ways to assess students' reading comprehension. You have to know your students and determine their abilities and learning styles. These projects have all been tested, but remember that each group of students will present new challenges that you will need to adjust to individually.

THE COMPUTER QUIZ

Since all students are created differently, you can use another method to assess students' after-reading comprehension during the school year.

For example, there is a software program called Scholastic Reading Counts. This is a program that offers book titles based on students' interests and Lexile levels. It tests students' reading comprehension with a ten-question quiz pulled from a pool of thirty questions, and it provides immediate feedback.

In addition, if the students are not able to earn a passing score the first time, it will allow them to retake the quiz with a different set of questions. It also allows teachers to access students' accounts in order to run reports and view quiz scores instantly!

Furthermore, students earn points for taking quizzes with a passing score. They can redeem those points with the person in charge (usually the media specialist), to choose rewards such as books, gadgets, and much more! However, this program does have costs, so you can research more about this option by going to the Scholastic Reading Counts website, teacher.scholastic.com/products/readingcounts.

The computer quiz is a good choice because some students do not like to do art-related projects, and some have enough homework to complete at home already—and this is an alternative after-reading assessment that they can complete during the school day. The quiz only takes ten to thirty minutes, depending on the student. It is an excellent way to monitor students' reading comprehension!

You usually have anywhere from five to ten students choose this option per literacy-group cycle, so you can send them to the computer lab in groups of three to four at the start or finish of class on the day everyone else turns in an after-reading project. It really works out great! If they have to take a quiz twice, you can average the two scores; but for the most part, students do well on the quizzes.

Unlike the projects, students can choose the computer quiz option as many times as they want throughout the literacy-group experience.

The reason this form of assessment is added is due to the scenario described throughout this book, the teacher notices a number of students with missing assignments, and most of those missing assignments are after-reading projects.

The teacher does not want to miss out on monitoring students' reading comprehension simply because students do not want to do a project at home, do not have the support to complete a project at home, or are already bogged down with other homework that takes precedence over a project (such as studying for a test for another class).

With this approach, students get the grade instead of a zero, and the teacher receives the data needed to monitor students' reading comprehension, to determine if learning, retention, and understanding are occurring. It works well for both the student and the teacher!

WHAT YOU HAVE LEARNED ABOUT AFTER READING

Students are like fingerprints: no two are the same! Thus, the way they learn, understand, and demonstrate mastery should be just as diverse. That is the motivation behind this assessment idea. You want students to feel your "student-centered" classroom for learning also means their evaluation offers choices.

Accordingly, their motivation to work in class increases because of all the choice given to them, and that makes you feel like it is all worth it! Yes, it takes extra time to grade projects versus multiple-choice tests, but the results are a true representation of learning, and the creativity is contagious. They are always trying to outdo the last project they completed, and that is what learners should always strive for—to better themselves.

Caroline confirms this approach: "I think that literacy groups are a very interesting thing to do because I liked to do the different roles. Another reason I liked literacy groups is the books that we get to choose from are good books, and after we are done reading the books, we get to do projects. Now, I think that is very interesting and different!"

The journey is coming to its end for the purpose of this text, but hopefully it is only the beginning for you. In the final chapter, you will discover the changes a teacher can make for the use of lit groups; so the journey will be taking a different path, and you will be left with many thoughts to consider.

So curl up on your couch one last time as you cruise through the final thoughts to consider in the last chapter; but do not be sad, because when you finish this book and close it for the last time, you get to embark on your own personal journey, which one day you will hopefully share with others.

6

Getting the Last Word In

"I like literacy groups! It gives us a chance to share what we think of the book and if you don't understand something, you can ask your team member. One of the things that I don't really like is the project choice because we weren't allowed to repeat the projects we enjoyed the most. I also think we should have more choices for our roles. I would also like more time during class for literacy groups. But, I really liked literacy groups overall," Sarah shares.

Well, you made it! You have hopefully laughed at some points and, at a few other points, shaken your head (in agreement); but overall, you have learned a lot through this journey. This has been a valuable journey through the use of literacy groups at the secondary-school level, and much ground has been covered in a short time! However, you are not finished just yet.

As Sarah so honestly points out, there are many areas in need for improvement, and that is exactly what this chapter discusses.

What could be different to make literacy groups more enjoyable, more productive, and more challenging for your students? How can you find out what your students truly think about what you are doing in the classroom, in order to have this type of self-reflection? These are valuable questions, so this chapter addresses the possible answers to these questions and more.

STUDENTS' OPINIONS

"I did not really like literacy groups, but I could have if I would have had more choice with picking my book, having more choice of roles, and allow me to make my own project ideas," Mitchell suggests.

Okay, face it, everyone has opinions, and adults oftentimes express those opinions whether other people want to hear them or not. Unfortunately, when it comes to your boss, you tend to keep those opinions bottled up, even if they could improve the atmosphere or improve productivity.

Well, the classroom is no different. School is a job for students, and you are their boss, so students do not always feel comfortable expressing their critical opinions to you. You can understand their reservations!

However, this text provides a way your students can share their opinions in a nonthreatening manner: an anonymous survey that you can give them at the end of the quarter, semester, or year. The idea was first used by a second-year teacher who moved from elementary to middle school because she wanted to be sure to make improvements each year, so the next group of students she was entrusted with would get a better version of a teacher.

Plus, like you, she understands that each year is a learning opportunity for her, and she should always look to grow and improve, to be the best she can be! This is true for most professionals, especially you!

The survey walks the students through a few questions pertaining to materials, lessons, activities, and the teacher's abilities. It has seven questions on it, so it does not take too long to administer. Please stress to your students the importance of the fact that they do not put their names on this paper.

In addition, so students feel comfortable being honest, do not walk around the room. When they finish, have them take the survey to the front of the classroom and slip it into an envelope. This way, you cannot match handwriting with the student, and the surveys get mixed up as the students put them into the envelope with other responses from all your classes.

It has been observed that teachers may sometimes get emotional when they read the surveys, because of the honesty behind every word. It will not always be positive, but it is certainly helpful.

It is the survey given in the scenario described throughout this text that inspired this chapter to consider the changes. (See appendix H for the survey.)

Although the survey does not specifically ask questions pertaining to literacy groups, the students generally comment on that particular experience because it consumes about half of their academic time in the classroom. For example, question 1 asks, "What was your most memorable lesson or activity this school year in class? Why?"

One student wrote, "I think the most memorable lesson or activity was literacy groups because it helped me to read more books than I would have. Now I am not scared to volunteer to read out loud."

Another student responded to the same question with a completely different answer: "The most memorable lesson or activity this year was when we played a bingo game, but you had to know the reading strategies and literal comprehension in order to play, and it was fun! Well fun for me because I knew the answers."

You can see the students truly take their time to respond thoughtfully to each question, and that makes them even more valuable. Then another questionnaire can be sent around asking students specifically about literacy groups; or you can simply add a question to the survey in the appendix.

For example, you could ask, "What do you think about the literacy-group experience?" Here is where you will receive the bulk of the feedback. This questionnaire may or may not be anonymous. Just remember people tend to be more honest when they don't have to put their name on it.

Recall from chapter 4 that "SIR" time is silent independent reading that students do twice a week for twenty minutes, in order to ensure that they receive practice with oral and silent reading, since oral and silent reading are two different cognitive skills. Plus, this allows you time to meet with students independently for about five minutes each.

Oral reading is the ability to read out loud with fluency and comprehension. It takes practice, and there are many ways students can practice this skill. They can read in front of a mirror or to someone younger. They can read into a tape recorder and play it back to self-reflect and make improvements. They can print out the lyrics to the latest song and practice reading them out loud with a friend.

On the other hand, silent reading is easy to practice by simply picking up a text and saying the words in your head. Silent reading can be practiced anywhere and anytime, like on a bus or during commercials. The bottom line is to practice both forms of reading.

Anne responds to the question about literacy groups with complete honesty: "I love the groups. I think they are fun and the reading goes by faster when you are with other people, and the projects are fun.

It doesn't seem like homework or work at all to me. The books I read this year were all great, and the people I worked with were great too. But the best part is that I read a lot of books this year and I'll still be reading more!"

This is not the opinion of all students. Remember, not every student will enjoy everything you do, no matter how student centered you make it. That is just the way it is in life.

For example, Trey's feelings are the opposite of Anne's. "I don't really like literacy group roles that much. I like the books, but there should be more roles to pick from." This supports the research and studies conducted over the past years in education: there is no one fix-all teaching idea that works for every student in every situation. But if you ever come across one, be sure to share it with the world.

THOUGHTS TO CONSIDER

An artist paints a picture and hangs it in a gallery. While it is displayed, it is criticized because in an observer's opinion there are things the artist could have done differently to continue to make the piece better.

Similarly, an author publishes a book and it is read by hundreds of people who make note of the details the author should add or remove to make the book better, less predictable, or more exciting. Needless to say, this is also the opinion of the readers.

The bottom line is that everything can use improvements and changes in order to constantly make it better, and the use of literacy groups is not any different. These suggestions for change come from many places, such as the students' surveys and questionnaire, additional research, and reflection from videotaping and audio recording of student-centered learning in the secondary content-area classrooms.

This section is simply food for thought to consider using during your journey through the use of literacy groups. This chapter is not implying that these changes must occur, but just think about it.

Text and Theme

The suggestions are broken down into the order of progression of use within the literacy-group experience. Thus the first point to consider is **texts and themes**.

First of all, you do not have to use novels. Literacy groups work just as well with learning geographical locations; in other words, have each group read text pertaining to a different place in the world and compile a final product that will teach the rest of the group about that location. You can even rotate the different locations so each group learns about it at some point during the year.

It works with a textbook too. For example, if you are a science teacher, and you are teaching students about classifying life, there may be four chapters in the textbook pertaining to this unit. You can use twenty minutes each day to give a minilesson on the skills for the unit and use thirty minutes for student-centered group learning.

One group can take chapter 14, on the structure of organisms, and another group can take chapter 15, on classifying living things. A third group can take chapter 16, which is about bacteria, and the fourth group can take chapter 17, which covers protists and fungi.

Each group is made up of five students. If you need an additional group, consider having one group responsible for research learning beyond the textbook. This is perfect for those higher-level-thinking students who need the extra challenge.

Once each group has read, studied, and learned their chapter using a strategy role, they create a way to deliver the information to the class. Or you might have them create new groups, where there is one expert from each group represented in the new group like a jigsaw activity. Either idea works perfectly for after-reading assessment. Now they share important details with the other group members.

This method of student-centered learning combined with daily minilessons is a surefire way to learn the content and enjoy the process at the same time.

Another point to consider that pertains to texts and themes is the possibility of allowing students to choose a theme and find a book or piece of text that represents that theme. This can be done after the first few cycles, once students grasp the routine and expectations.

Allow your students to choose topics or themes connected to your subject's standards or learning goals, and then take your students to the media center, where the media specialist can assist them with locating the appropriate text (article, book, or website). The best part about this type of learning is it is student centered, which usually increases interest and motivation to learn.

Group Discussion

When someone earns a master's degree, she or he is required to discuss research and synthesize information. This allows your mind to take in the new information, process it by making connections and drawing conclusions, and then permanently store it in your long-term memory. This is a very important skill to have, and students should be exposed to it early on to ensure mastery.

Thus this next suggestion, **group discussion**, is to allow groups to regroup after they finish reading the text, to discuss and synthesize common themes, support opinions, and analyze similarities and differences. This entire cooperative learning process is supported by years of solid research (Johnson, Johnson, and Holubec 1994; Kagan 2001).

In other words, if you have five groups, have one student from each group come together to form a new discussion group. Now the new group has one person representing group 1, one person from group 2, one person from group 3, one person from group 4, and one person from group 5, which is referred to as a jigsaw activity.

This instructional method is a great way to practice important skills, get to know new classmates, and hear about other texts in order to gain a greater understanding of material and expand perspectives. It is also a heterogeneous way to group students, as well as provide differentiated instruction, all within a cooperative learning atmosphere.

Time Management

Another thought regards the **time management** of the cooperative-learning experience. You should consider the idea of extending the amount of time allotted for reading the books or texts, depending what you choose to use.

If you choose to use poems, short stories, chapters from a textbook, magazine articles, or newspapers, you can very easily stay on the two-week schedule without feeling rushed. You may even want to use just a week, depending on the depth of the material you desire to cover.

Conversely, for the use of novels, switching to a three-week schedule allows the students more class time for discussion, group and re-group interaction, teacher-guided small-group instruction, and much more. By adjusting your time based on students' needs you are able to better customize your content to promote that student-centered, cooperative-learning environment.

Furthermore, this idea of more time with the novel also goes with providing more classroom support and less homework responsibility. There can be a day dedicated to student after-reading assessment. It can be referred to as "Student Workshop Day."

With more and more parents working and being out of the home, it is difficult for students to receive the structure, supplies, and support that are needed in order for homework to be beneficial. The students can still do some reading at home, along with fulfilling their roles, but they will receive even more student-teacher interaction through the extended class time.

An extra week will also mean every student receives one-on-one time with the teacher, instead of just twelve out of twenty-three, and every group receives the important small-group instruction with every novel, instead of just four out of five. It actually sounds perfect! You can also consider offering before- and after-school assistance for students who need additional support.

Project Choices

One of the main complaints students have with school is being bored with doing the same thing over and over again. They are not referring to the structure or consistency, but to the lack of options for learning—they're talking about things like always taking notes to receive information or always previewing a chapter to activate prior knowledge.

It has been said that doing the same thing day after day and lesson after lesson can appear boring to any person of any age. Think back to your own experiences while attending classes as a student. That is why you can change how you teach and the order in which you teach strategies and skills every year! Students deserve the same respect.

Therefore, another possibility to consider is allowing students to repeat **project choices** more than once. In the scenario described throughout this text, the teacher only allows the students to complete each project one time, but that can be changed to many different options.

One option is to let students choose any project up to two or three times, after which they must challenge themselves with a different after-reading assessment.

The full-fledged version of that idea is to let students choose whatever projects they wish to, without any limits on how many times they can complete a certain project. You can always wait to make this decision until the students are able to give their input, which will only bolster the student-centered environment that you are trying to nurture.

One possibility to ponder is that of limiting the number of copies of each rubric to the number of students you have. This will ensure that each student only completes the project one time. For example, if you have a total of 120 students, then you will only make 120 copies of the map rubric, 120 of the character-bookmark rubrics, and so on.

New Roles

It is common for students to request a greater selection of literacy roles to choose from. The only problem with this suggestion is that it requires more modeling, practicing, and mastering of new strategies.

However, to show your students you value them, it may be worth the extra time of teaching **new roles**. Plus, you can alternate your instructional time between teaching and practicing literal- and critical-comprehension skills, on the one hand, and, on the other, presenting new literacy roles that will assist students in being better readers of your content. Here are a few alternative strategies that can also be used as literacy-group roles.

The first reading strategy to consider as a possible role is *prediction*. Making predictions is an easy strategy to master. The reader uses prior knowledge, pictures, charts, figures, graphs, titles, subtitles, and any text read to make an educated guess or prediction about what happens next in the text.

A good way to introduce making predictions is to use a picture book. Read the title and talk about the picture on the cover. Then read the synopsis on the back of the book. Finally, make a prediction statement, which starts with "I think . . ." or "I believe . . ." Keep in mind that predictions can change as information is presented. Continue to do this think-aloud throughout the entire read-aloud.

Follow the same gradual-release or scaffolding system explained in chapter 4. Provide the students with a whole-class practice, small-group practice, partner practice, and individual practice, all with teacher guidance as needed. This supports the "I do," "we do," "they do," and "you do" model. Last but not least, give the strategy a catchy name, such as "psychic predictor," for its use as a literacy-group role.

Another reading strategy to consider as a possible literacy-group role is *summarizing*. This would be a great role because of the importance behind the strategy. Even Richard Allington (2006) defines summarizing as the essential component to learning.

Summarizing is a wonderful way to restate what has happened in the text. Summarizing allows the student to record key events that are important to remember in order to maintain comprehension. Of course, you should model and practice summarizing with the students over a few days. You can use a picture book to introduce the new strategy or skill because it is less threatening for the students. Finally, give the strategy a great title, such as "reader's digest."

Since *learning new vocabulary* is important for all ages, this can be a role for literacy groups too. A student can be responsible for identifying one to three unfamiliar words or important words from each night's scheduled reading.

The student can record the word, write the sentence in which it was found, write the definition that closely represents the way the word was used, and think of an example, illustration, or synonym to further the understanding of the word. Maybe he or she can create an interactive game for the group members to play in order to make the word move from just a word to something personal. That can depend on the importance of the word.

Definitely be sure to model and practice this strategy of monitoring unfamiliar words. You may even want to do a lesson pertaining to context clues, so students have ways to help themselves when presented with unfamiliar words at home or in other situations where there may not be anyone around to help with the meaning of the word.

Janet Allen (1999) agrees that teachers need to model the proper way to use the text, in addition to other strategies for understanding new words. This modeling process is best done using the think-aloud method, which provides students with the experience and examples to use when they are one their own encountering unfamiliar words.

What is more, having students think aloud and talk through difficult text is an instructional strategy that helps students become active learners who are able to personalize what the class has to offer. Through this method of instruction, the students experience a wide range of text and resources to assist in building new meaning and understanding of the world around them in relation to your content area (Blachowicz and Fisher, 2006).

Finally, give it a cool name, such as "speech booster." I know that sources on the Internet call this role "vocabulary enricher," which can be another title option.

Students can also do something as simple as *making comments.* This is an easy strategy because, as people, we constantly make personal comments about the world around us. These comments generally are connected to emotions, so they represent feelings. This strategy allows students to express their likes, dislikes, points of agreement, and points of disagreement with respect to a text.

Remember, some strategies may need more practice than others, so you need to make that call based on the needs of your students. A good name for this role is "passionate critic."

Another piece of food for thought is the suggestion that a student might be responsible for identifying whatever element the class is focusing on. For example, say you are teaching the students literal comprehension, and they are specifically learning how to identify a main idea.

One student in the group can be responsible for recording the main idea of the reading selection for each assigned reading.

What a great way to incorporate skills with strategies and have a well-rounded small-group discussion pertaining to all the important aspects of being a good reader. It will also allow you to monitor students' ability to master locating and stating a main idea.

Ideally, this role can change with each skill they are working on in class, such as providing supporting details or identifying an *implied* main idea. It will also work with critical-comprehension skills, such as determining an author's tone and purpose or comparing and contrasting.

Plus, with you modeling and practicing, it will already be included in your teach time or minilesson—because it is what the whole class is trying to master anyway. Think about the possibilities of this literacy role. You can have students monitor text for key points to support a textbook chapter or key concepts that you are working on in any subject area. You can call this role "skill builder."

After-Reading Project Choices

A final possibility to consider is adding more **after-reading project choices** for the students to pick from. Of course, it is not about how many they have to choose from, but the fact that there are different types of projects to meet their individual styles so they can express their understanding of the book in a creative way that meets their needs.

The after-reading project/assessment is how you can easily differentiate your evaluation method for your students. Thus, in the next section you will read about further research to develop even more after-reading assessment options.

One additional project can be the *cereal-box book report*, which several teachers use as a culminating project in their classrooms.

The project has students create a cereal box out of the important details and facts from the book. The students should include the title of the book in a cereal-box format, such as "Harry Potter Puffs," and include the author's name. On the side of the box, the students should include "nutrition facts," using the characters and percentage figures representing how often the characters are included in the book. For example, Harry Potter appears in the story 100 percent of the time.

Below the nutrition facts, the students should include a short summary of the book. On the other side of the box, the students should include questions and answers pertaining to the book. Finally, on the back of the box, the students should include an interactive puzzle, game, or maze related to the idea of the book. Some other ideas that should be included to make the cereal box more authentic are a mail-in offer for a toy, an advertisement to promote the book, or a cartoon based on the book. (See appendix I for the new project rubrics.) This is a wonderful idea for science and social-studies classes especially.

Another project that can be added to the list of choices is the *historical newspaper*. For this project, students use different events that occur in the book to formulate short articles for a one- to two-page historical newspaper. They use tea bags to age the paper and just a have a lot of fun with it.

For example, if the students are reading *Bud, Not Buddy*, by Christopher Paul Curtis, then they may want to write a short article on jazz, one on the Great Depression, and one on the difficult times African Americans faced during that time period. The possibilities for this project in the context of social-studies classes are endless!

With media taking over students' attention nowadays, why not have the next few projects pertain to media? For example, students could create a *movie poster* advertising their book. It can be fun, entertaining, and productive.

The poster can have the book title, author, and release date. It can have a wonderful illustration of the main idea or theme, with a short sentence or two across it. This can be a wonderful way to express their knowledge of the book.

Also, the students can create a *song about the book*. The students can use all the key ideas, themes, or events to write a short song that represents the overall story of the book. They can title the song with the book title and author, and create a chorus that depicts the problem or conflict in the story.

To take it a step further, your students can record their voices singing their song as a final product. These are two additional project choices to consider.

Open-mind portraits, adapted from *Fifty Literacy Strategies*, by Gail Tompkins (1998), can be an after-reading assessment choice to consider using. This project is perfect for the student who has the character-captain role or for a class studying a person from history. This project requires students to truly consider the main character of the story from every perspective.

The students draw a head and neck of the main character to start with. On the front of the head, the students draw in the details of the character's features (hair, eyes, nose, ears, etc.). On the other side (the "mind"), the students draw images to depict key feelings and thoughts from the story that are connected to the main character (Tompkins 1998, 71–72). Figure 6.1 is an example of what the cutout for the open-mind-portrait project looks like.

There is also the option of allowing your students to complete a WebQuest. This is an Internet guide through a topic that allows

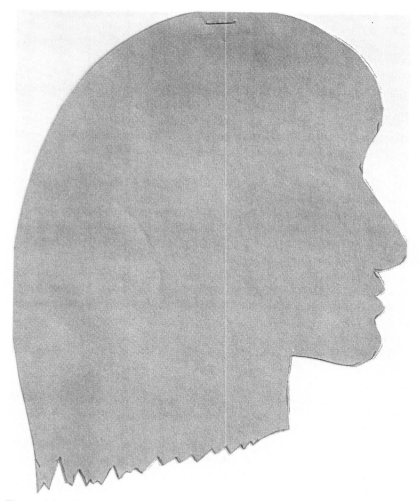

Figure 6.1.   Sample Open-Mind

students to demonstrate mastery using websites and other references. Many WebQuests have been created by educators on a broad range of topics and novels, and you may use these with your students. Additionally, you can create your own WebQuest specific to your topic and grade level.

A WebQuest is a site that students go to, where they follow guidelines or directions to reach a personal learning outcome. Most WebQuests start students out with an *introduction*. This is where a purpose is established for the assignment. Then the students move forward to a *task*. In this section, students discover the steps they will take to reach the learning outcome.

Next, students follow a *process*. The process is where they conduct research, read from different resources, analyze information, and gather useful facts and data.

Afterward, they are given an *evaluation*. In this phase, the student uses a rubric to finalize, summarize, and self-reflect on his or her experience though the WebQuest assignment. Finally, the student is able to finish the process in the *conclusion* phase, which provides additional sites, games, and so on for the students to enjoy. A great website to help you get started incorporating this idea is the San Diego State University site, www.webquest.org/index.php.

Basically, the possibilities for after reading-assessment are limitless. There are so many creative ways to evaluate students' comprehension that it is utterly amazing.

Some additional ideas to explore are *quilts, comic strips, iMoves, PowerPoint presentations,* and *reader's-theater skits.* If you are still looking for more ideas, visit www.litcircles.org/Extension/extension .html for extension projects that are not listed or explained within this book; or ask the student to create a project and grading rubric.

THE FINAL WORD

Well, you have reached your destination: giving students a safe atmosphere where discussion occurs about all different types of text. It has definitely been a journey worth experiencing.

Remember, literacy groups are not a fix-all teaching method to get all students to become proficient readers. But using literacy groups provides the students with choice, which inspires them to participate, read an abundance of text, and better master the skills connected to your subject area.

In addition, it is a wonderful way to expose students to different forms of text to learn from and to break up the reading in a chapter, in order to decrease the overwhelming feeling sometimes felt from textbook reading.

Furthermore, several students shared that they would have never even read one book in a year, much less fifteen books. Even more importantly, most students found authors or genres that have motivated them to continue reading.

For example, Michael read *The Lightning Thief*, by Rick Riordan, which is a book about Greek mythology written in an action-and-adventure style, and this turned Michael on to other action-and-adventure books, such as the Ranger's Apprentice series by John Flanagan. This is what trying something new is all about!

Remember this journey is explained using a scenario intended to be implemented as a guide for all those who come along for the ride through the description provided throughout this professional text. It should be used as a cooperative-learning guide to help you adapt literacy groups into a workable teaching method that meets the needs of your student population and subject area.

For example, if you teach drama and you want to help your students discover the importance and use of fluency and voice, you could use literacy groups to serve this purpose.

Simply have each group start off by listening to an audio recording of a book being read. Ask each member of the group to record the qualities that he or she feels permit an actor to demonstrate fluency and voice. Then allow them to share their notes with the whole class. Next, give each group a short movie clip to watch and complete a different task.

Finally, have the students read a short play and practice fluency and voice within their small groups. It really makes a difference to work in small learning groups or literacy groups, versus whole-class instruction.

Moreover, you want your students to see your love and passion for reading to learn your content area and to be overwhelmed with the same joy. You want students to feel like they can overcome reading struggles by listening to you as you share your limitations and think aloud, thereby demonstrating how to get unstuck when meaning breaks down.

Many teachers have experienced the following phenomenon: if the teacher is excited about what is going on in the classroom, then the students are also excited about learning in the classroom.

It is for all these reasons and more that you have chosen to read this book, so now is the time to get creative and try literacy groups within your content area. The worst thing that can happen is it does not work perfectly on the first attempt, so there is nothing to lose. You are in the best profession to continue to grow and develop right alongside the students. Seize the day!

Simply take the time to listen to your students, and you will know without a doubt that using literacy groups or some type of cooperative learning is what is best for your classroom.

The students presented in the scenario have more than expressed their enjoyment with the use of literacy groups throughout the school year. Therefore, it is only right to end this journey with the voices of the students who make this experience possible, because they are the reasons to take your own journey with your students.

"I think literacy-group roles are a great idea because they teach you to discuss what is happening in the book. They also get students in groups with different people," Kevin expresses.

"I love the whole point of literacy groups because it helps students learn about how to do their role in their journal during and after reading. I also love literacy groups because you get to experience different genres and change up the variety of books you read," Alexis shares.

"After every two weeks of literacy books, when we come back to school, I love getting new books and then reading them in class. It is a great way to get to know other people and a great way to see what others like about the book," Brad notes.

"I think that the literacy groups are very fun! I also like that in the groups there are roles that you can talk about with other students. So I really enjoyed the overall experience of literacy groups," Dillon expresses.

Last but not least, Tom states, "I think the groups are very good to interact with people that enjoy the same book as you," which makes discussion and learning all the more worth it. Now, go give this form of cooperative learning a try, and create a testimony of your own about the experience of using literacy groups with your students and your subject area, in your classroom. Good luck!

Appendix A

Book List and Reading Schedule

The following is the book list referred to in the scenario for literacy groups. It is intended to provide teachers with a basis to start using literacy groups within their classrooms. This is just a sample of themes and topics, so please feel free to adapt or change it to fit your individual subject area and students' needs. Remember, you can choose to use chapters from a textbook, magazines, newspapers, poems, and so on. The material choices are limitless.

Table A.1. Book List and Reading Schedule

Dates	Theme	Book	Author	Genre	Pages	Lexile
2nd: 9/10–9/23	War	My Brother Sam Is Dead	Collier	Historical Fiction	216	770
6th: 11/5–11/18		The Red Badge of Courage	Crane	Classic Fiction	138	920
4th: 1/22–2/3		The Gods of Mars	Burroughs	Fiction	247	1050
3rd: 4/14–4/25		Heroes Don't Run	Mazer	Historical Fiction	128	650
		Across Five Aprils	Hunt	Historical Fiction	190	1100
3rd: 9/10–9/23	Human struggle	Harriet Tubman	Petry	Nonfiction	242	1000
2nd: 11/5–11/18		Roll of Thunder, Hear My Cry	Taylor	Historical Fiction	210	920
6th: 1/22–2/3		Under the Same Sky	DeFelice	Realistic Fiction	224	750
4th: 4/14–4/25		Narrative Life of F. Douglass	Douglass	Autobiography	122	700
		Anne Frank	Falstein	Nonfiction	92	500
4th: 9/10–9/23	Holocaust	Daniel's Story	Matas	Nonfiction	131	720
3rd: 11/5–11/18		Number the Stars	Lowry	Nonfiction	137	670
2nd: 1/22–2/3		Surviving Hitler	Warren	Nonfiction	216	820
6th: 4/14–4/25		Night	Wiesel	Nonfiction	120	590
		I Am Star	Auerbacher	Nonfiction	96	500
6th: 9/10–9/23	Ghosts	Lily's Ghost	Ruby	Fiction	258	710
4th: 11/5–11/18		The Old Willis Place	Hahn	Fiction	199	630
3rd: 1/22–2/3		The Ghost Sitter	Griffin	Fiction	131	700
2nd: 4/14–4/25		The Ghost's Grave	Kehret	Fiction	210	790
		Ghost Hotel	Weinberg	Fiction	176	850

Period	Theme	Title	Author	Genre		
2nd: 9/24–10/7	Loss/death	Sadako & the Thousand Paper	Coerr	Nonfiction	65	630
6th: 11/19–12/2		Mick Harte Was Here	Park	Realistic Fiction	89	730
4th: 2/4–2/17		Tears of a Tiger	Draper	Realistic Fiction	180	700
3rd: 4/28–5/9		Listening for Lions	Whelan	Fiction	194	900
		Fever 1793	Anderson	Fiction	251	580
3rd: 9/24–10/7	Survival	The Boy Who Spoke Dog	Morgan	Fiction	166	650
2nd: 11/19–12/2		Julie of the Wolves	George	Classic Fiction	170	860
6th: 2/4–2/17		Brian's Winter	Paulsen	Fiction	144	1140
4th: 4/28–5/9		Hatchet	Paulsen	Fiction	208	1020
		Overboard	Fama	Fiction	158	690
4th: 9/24–10/7	Mystery	Chasing Vermeer	Balliet	Fiction	254	770
3rd: 11/19–12/2		Skeleton Man	Bruchac	Fiction	114	730
2nd: 2/4–2/17		Things Not Seen	Clements	Fiction	251	690
6th: 4/28–5/9		The Anybodies	Bode	Fiction	276	730
		Mystery of the Island Jewels	Stengel	Fiction	208	500
6th: 9/24–10/7	(Auto)biography	All Creatures Great and Small	Herriot	Nonfiction	499	990
4th: 11/19–12/2		Ben and Me	Lawson	Nonfiction	114	1010
3rd: 2/4–2/17		True Confessions of a Heartless Girl	Brooks	Nonfiction	216	740
2nd: 4/28–5/9		Everyday Heroes	Johnson	Nonfiction	167	600
		Reading Changed My Life	Johnson	Nonfiction	94	700

(continued)

Table A.I. (continued)

Dates	Theme	Book	Author	Genre	Pages	Lexile
2nd: 10/8–10/21	Historical fiction	Quake!	Karwoski	Historical Fiction	153	770
6th: 12/3–12/16		The Golden Hour	Williams	Historical Fiction	259	740
4th: 2/19–3/2		Bud, Not Buddy	Curtis	Historical Fiction	272	950
3rd: 5/12–5/25		House of the Red Fish	Salisbury	Historical Fiction	304	610
		When My Name Was Keoko	Park	Historical Fiction	196	610
3rd: 10/8–10/21	Nonfiction	Double Life of Pocahontas	Fritz	Nonfiction	96	910
2nd: 12/3–12/16		Letters My Mother Never Read	Sueck	Nonfiction	199	950
6th: 2/19–3/2		The Big Wave	Buck	Nonfiction	57	790
4th: 5/12–5/25		Farewell to Manzanar	Houston	Nonfiction	185	1040
		The Wright Brothers at Kitty Hawk	Sobol	Nonfiction	122	570
4th: 10/8–10/21	Bullying	The Gun	Langan	Realistic Fiction	123	750
3rd: 12/3–12/16		The Bully	Langan	Realistic Fiction	190	700
2nd: 2/19–3/2		Bullying in School	Langan	Nonfiction	52	500
6th: 5/12–5/25		Tangerine	Bloor	Realistic Fiction	312	680
		Freak the Mighty	Philibrick	Realistic Fiction	176	1000
6th: 10/8–10/21	Realistic fiction	Lost and Found	Schraff	Realistic Fiction	133	760
4th: 12/3–12/16		Shiloh Season	Naylor	Realistic Fiction	128	860
3rd: 2/19–3/2		Brothers in Arms	Langan	Realistic Fiction	152	800
2nd: 5/12–5/25		Jackie's Wild Seattle	Hobbs	Realistic Fiction	200	660
		Chicken Boy	Dowell	Realistic Fiction	202	860

Schedule	Category	Title	Author	Genre	Pages	Lexile
2nd: 10/22–11/4	Classics	The Secret Garden	Verney	Classic Fiction	284	410
6th: 1/8–1/20		The Scarlet Letter	Hawthorne	Classic Fiction	202	1340
4th: 3/24–4/4		Adventures of Tom Sawyer	Twain	Classic Fiction	319	900
3rd: 5/26–6/8		The Talking Earth	George	Classic Fiction	151	770
		Return to Hawk's Hill	Eckert	Classic Fiction	204	1230
3rd: 10/22–11/4	Action/adventure	Heir Apparent	Vande Velde	Fantasy Fiction	336	820
2nd: 1/8–1/20		Chasing the Falconers	Korman	Fiction	160	680
6th: 3/24–4/4		Harry Potter & the Chamber of Secrets	Rowling	Fantasy Fiction	341	940
4th: 5/26–6/8		The Lightning Thief	Riordan	Myth Fiction	400	740
		Rising Water	Petersen	Fiction	128	480
4th: 10/22–11/4	"Kids like me"	Surviving the Applewhites	Tolan	Fiction	216	820
3rd: 1/8–1/20		6th Grade Can Really Kill You	DeClements	Realistic Fiction	146	700
2nd: 3/24–4/4		How to Disappear Completely and Never Be Found	Nickerson	Fiction	281	720
6th: 5/26–6/8		Drums, Girls, and Dangerous Pie	Sonnenblick	Realistic Fiction	304	940
		Double Dutch	Draper	Realistic Fiction	183	760
6th: 10/22–11/4	Fantasy/fairy tales	Artemis Fowl (book 1)	Colfer	Fiction	279	600
4th: 1/8–1/20		Once Upon a Marigold	Ferris	Fiction	266	840
3rd: 3/24–4/4		Peter and the Starcatchers	Barry	Fiction	480	770
2nd: 5/26–6/8		The Unseen	Snyder	Fiction	199	990
		Gregor the Overlander	Collins	Fiction	311	630

Appendix B

Question-Answer
Relationship Cycle

This is to provide teachers with a visual for teaching question-answer relationship (QAR), so students can have a clear understanding of question types. You can even have students create their own QAR visuals. This is adapted from several sources.

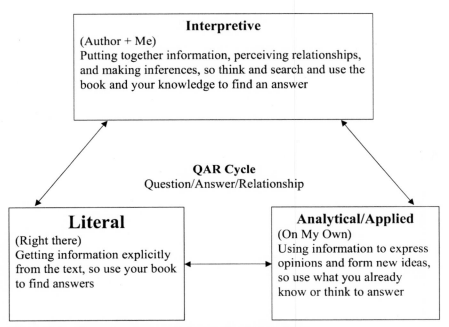

Figure B.1.   Question-Answer Relationship (QAR) Cycle

Appendix C

Visualizing Handout

This document is for the teacher's use with visualizing. It can be given to each student as a graphic organizer or simply made into a transparency. You could also laminate a few copies to reuse in a center with dry-erase markers.

Name _____ Date _____ Class _____

Directions: Listen to a story or read a story and allow your mind to create visual images or pictures of what is happening based on the words the author uses to provoke your mind's eye. Draw the images you see at four different points in the story or text. Remember to add as much detail as possible, just as the author uses many descriptive words to paint the picture for you.

Table C.1.   Visualizing Handout

Visualizing	

Appendix D

Character-Analysis Web

This web is used as a graphic organizer to help students learn the process of character evaluation. This is simply a tool and can be adapted or used to meet the needs of your individual students.

Character Analysis Web

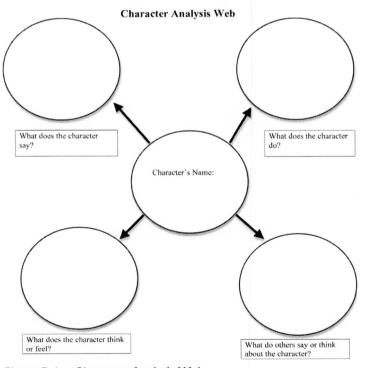

What does the character say?

What does the character do?

Character's Name:

What does the character think or feel?

What do others say or think about the character?

Figure D.1. Character-Analysis Web

Appendix E

Reading Schedule

There are two different forms of the reading schedule: one works with a two-week (ten-day) duration, and one is for a three-week (fifteen-day) period. You may want to vary the schedule based on the length of the text, the difficulty of the text, or the student's reading rate. This form is adapted from *Literature Circles*, by Pat Elliott and Dale Mays (2001).

Table E.1.   Reading Schedule

Reading Schedule

Book Title: _____

Date:	Pages:
Date: _____	Pages: _____
Date: _____	Pages: _____
Date: _____	Pages: _____
Date: _____	Pages: _____
Date: _____	Pages: _____
Date: _____	Pages: _____
Date: _____	Pages: _____
Date: _____	Pages: _____
Date: _____	Pages: _____
Date: _____	Pages: _____

Reading Schedule

Book Title: _____

Date:	Pages:
Date: _____	Pages: _____
Date: _____	Pages: _____
Date: _____	Pages: _____
Date: _____	Pages: _____
Date: _____	Pages: _____
Date: _____	Pages: _____
Date: _____	Pages: _____
Date: _____	Pages: _____
Date: _____	Pages: _____
Date: _____	Pages: _____

Appendix F

After-Reading-Project Rubrics

These rubrics are provided as a sample to get you started with creating your own. Rubrics should guide students in their ability to express their knowledge of the text they read. It is important to allow students to use a rubric while creating a project.

CD COVER[1] (100 POINTS)

_____ Illustrate the key concept from the text on both sides of the CD case. **(10 points)**

_____ The cover needs the book title and the number one song title on the front. **(10 points)**

_____ The cover should have an eye catching illustration, not stick figures. **(15 points)**

_____ The back needs at least 10 songs minimum that capture key events. **(30 points)**

_____ Must be put in an actual CD case. **(10 points)**

_____ Your name, the due date, and the period must be present. **(6 points)**

_____ It must be neat, colorful, and organized. **(19 points)**

_____ **Total points earned**

COLLAGE[2] (100 POINTS)

_____ Design a random collection of figures that represent key concepts in the text using multiple media sources, such as personal photos, hand drawings (not stick figures), or Internet-sourced art/clip art. **(25 points)**

_____ Then describe what each figure represents and how it relates to the key concept of the text on the back side of the collage or separate sheet of paper; be sure to answer the "so what?" **(30 points)**

_____ Must fill the page completely. **(19 points)**

_____ Include the book title and author. **(6 points)**

_____ Your name, the due date, and the period must be present. **(6 points)**

_____ It must be neat, colorful, and organized. **(14 points)**

_____ **Total points earned**

CHARACTER BOOKMARK³ (100 POINTS)

_____ Design a life size bookmark that depicts the main person of the text. **(20 points)**

_____ You should have the title and author of the text. Also include the name of the person and a drawing of the person (not a stick figure). **(20 points)**

_____ On the reverse side, write a character analysis which should include your opinion of the character with support and why you chose him or her; be sure to answer the "so what?" **(40 points)**

_____ Your name, the due date, and the period must be present. **(6 points)**

_____ It must be neat, colorful, and organized. **(14 points)**

_____ **Total points earned**

GAME BOARD[4] (100 POINTS)

_____ Invent a game based on your text/book that represents key ideas. **(20 points)**

_____ People who play your game must use knowledge gained from the text to do well. **(10 points)**

_____ Include the book title, author, and name for the game. **(15 points)**

_____ Directions should be included and written clearly. **(20 points)**

_____ Game pieces should be included. **(15 points)**

_____ Your name, the due date, and the period must be present. **(6 points)**

_____ It must be neat, colorful, and organized. **(14 points)**

_____ **Total points earned**

MAP[5] (100 POINTS)

_____ Design a map to record the journey of the main person's life (i.e. actual movement or mental movement). **(20 points)**

_____ The journey needs to demonstrate the most important movements connected to the big idea or message of the text. **(30 points)**

_____ Include a legend or key to explain the map symbols. **(18 points)**

_____ Include the book title and author, and name the journey. **(6 points)**

_____ Your name, the due date, and the period must be present. **(6 points)**

_____ It must be neat, colorful, and organized. **(20 points)**

_____ **Total points earned**

LETTER TO YOUR AUTHOR (100 POINTS)

_____ Research is evident and provided with the letter. **(10 points)**

_____ Write a letter to your author introducing who you are (DO NOT include your last name), where you go to school, and why you are writing to him or her. **(10 points)**

_____ Then describe some cool facts you've learned about him or her through your research. **(10 points)**

_____ Next, talk about what you liked about the book you read. **(10 points)**

_____ Finally, conclude with a thank-you and the hope that you'll hear from the author soon. **(10 points)**

_____ You must type your final letter. **(10 points)**

_____ It should not have more than five grammatical errors. **(10 points)**

_____ It should make sense and sound right and look right. Are paragraphs formed for each idea? **(10 points)**

_____ You should provide an envelope for your letter to be mailed in after it is graded. **(10 points)**

_____ The research has the student's name, the due date, and the period written on the top page and is stapled together. **(10 points)**

_____ **Total Points Earned**

PICTURE BOOK OF THE NOVEL (100 POINTS)

Decide what are the most important events that occurred in the novel. Illustrate each important event with a drawing, clip art, an Internet picture, or an image from a magazine. Then pair the illustration with written text so it imitates a picture-book style.

_____ There is a cover present with the title of the book, the author's name, and an illustration. **(6 points)**

_____ There is a title page present with your name, the period, and the due date. **(4 points)**

_____ Each page has an illustration and text to support the picture. **(15 points)**

_____ At least twenty important events are clearly written, with lots of detail and description. **(15 points)**

_____ The text is neatly written or typed. **(10 points)**

_____ There are fewer than five grammatical errors (spelling, punctuation, etc.). **(10 points)**

_____ The picture book is bound together by some method other than stapling or paper-clipping. **(10 points)**

_____ The illustrations demonstrate effort and do not employ stick figures. **(10 points)**

_____ Each page is numbered. **(10 points)**

_____ Pencil is not used anywhere in the picture book. **(10 points)**

_____ **Total Points Earned**

SCRAPBOOK OF MAIN CHARACTER (100 POINTS)

Decide what are the most important events that occurred in the main character's life. Illustrate each event with a drawing, clip art, an Internet picture, or an image from a magazine. Create speech bubbles, with text representing the main character's thoughts or feelings.

_____ The scrapbook has the title, author, student's name, due date, and period on the cover. **(8 points)**

_____ The scrapbook demonstrates a sequence of events in the order in which they occurred. **(20 points)**

_____ Every part of the main character's life is present on some page of the scrapbook. **(20 points)**

_____ The bubble text is neatly written and not crammed into the bubble. **(8 points)**

_____ There are fewer than five grammatical errors (spelling, punctuation, etc.). **(8 points)**

_____ The scrapbook is bound together by some method other than stapling or paper-clipping. **(8 points)**

_____ The illustrations demonstrate effort and do not employ stick figures. **(8 points)**

_____ Pencil is not used anywhere in the scrapbook. **(8 points)**

_____ The scrapbook represents the true look of a photo-album scrapbook. **(8 points)**

_____ It is neat, colorful, and organized. **(4 points)**

_____ **Total Points Earned**

BOOK-BOX PROJECT (100 POINTS)

_____ Decorate the outside of a box by covering the entire piece. **(20 points)**

_____ The main idea or theme, the book title, the author's name, the student's name, the date, and the period should be presented creatively around the outside of the box. **(20 points)**

_____ Collect five objects or pictures related to a story, informational book, or novel and put them in a box. **(20 points)**

_____ The Book Inventory Checklist should be attached to the lid of the box and filled out with the required information (what each item is and why it was worth putting in the box). **(20 points)**

_____ The box must represent effort, neatness, color, and organization. **(20 points)**

_____ **Total points earned**

BOOK-BOX INVENTORY CHECKLIST

1. The Book, _____

    WHY? _____

2. _____

    WHY? _____

3. _____

    WHY? _____

4. _____

    WHY? _____

5. _____

    WHY? _____

NOTES

1. From Schlick Noe, Literature Circles Resource Center, "CD Cover," © 2002. http://www.litcircles.org/Extension/cd.html. Used by permission.

2. From Schlick Noe, Literature Circles Resource Center, "Collage," © 2002. http://www.litcircles.org/Extension/cd.html. Used by permission.

3. From Schlick Noe, Literature Circles Resource Center, "Character Bookmark," © 2002. http://www.litcircles.org/Extension/cd.html. Used by permission.

4. From Schlick Noe, Literature Circles Resource Center, "Game Board," © 2002. http://www.litcircles.org/Extension/cd.html. Used by permission.

5. From Schlick Noe, Literature Circles Resource Center, "Map," © 2002. http://www.litcircles.org/Extension/cd.html. Used by permission.

Appendix G

Text-Review Form

This form is similar to a cloze passage, which guides the students to write a review on a text they have read. This form is adapted from *The Skilled Reader*, by Susan G. Pongratz (2005).

Figure G.1.   Text-Review Form

Text Review

As you fill in the cloze document, be sure to include details, support from the text, and your opinion and reasoning for each answer.

Name _____ Due Date _____ Class _____

Title of Text: _____

Author: _____

Rating: 1   2   3   4   5   6   7   8   9   10

Key Point / Main Idea: _____
_____

This text describes whom? _____
_____.

As the text develops, _____
_____.

This text clearly depicts _____.

The strength of the text represented by _____.

For example, _____
_____.

However, one weakness the text has is _____
_____.

Overall, _____
_____.

Appendix H

Student Survey

This survey will provide you with the feedback to improve your students' learning environment and your teaching ability.

CLASSROOM SURVEY

Directions: *This survey is anonymous. Please be honest and provide constructive criticism. Read each question carefully and answer in a complete sentence.*

1. What was your most memorable lesson or activity up to this point in class? Why?

   _____

   _____

2. What lesson or activity would you suggest I change for next year? Why?

   _____

   _____

3. What was your favorite text you read this year in class? Why?

   _____

   _____

4. What was your favorite text you read on your own that you would like to recommend I use in future classes? Why and how will it fit in with the class?

   _____

   _____

5. On a scale from 1 to 10 (1 being the lowest-not good and 10 being the highest-excellent), how would you rate your teacher's ability to explain new concepts to you? Why?

   _____

   _____

6. On a scale from 1 to 10 (1 being the lowest-not good and 10 being the highest-excellent), how would you rate your teacher's ability to listen and answer your questions during class discussion? Why?

   _____

   _____

7. What changes would you make to the overall classroom structure within this class? Why?

   _____

   _____

Appendix I

Chapter 6
Additional Project Rubrics

The following rubrics are provided for you to use and adapt in addition to the original project suggestions.

CEREAL-BOX BOOK PROJECT (100 POINTS)

_____ Cover the whole box with colorful paper. (**10 points**)
_____ The project is colorful and appealing to the eye. (**10 points**)
_____ The project is neatly done. (**10 points**)
_____ The project includes the title of the book and the author on the front. (**10 points**)
_____ There is an illustration present on the front. (**10 points**)
_____ The nutrition facts (character list) and book summary are present on one side of the box. (**10 points**)
_____ The questions and answers are present on the other side. (**10 points**)
_____ The project includes a puzzle, game, OR maze on the back of the box. (**10 points**)
_____ The project has one extra: mail-in offer, advertisement of book, OR cartoon based on the book. (**10 points**)
_____ The student's name, the due date, and the period are located at the bottom of the back side of the box. (**10 points**)
_____ **Total points earned**

OPEN-MIND PORTRAITS (100 POINTS)

_____ Draw and color a portrait of the head and neck of the main character from the book. **(20 points)**

_____ Cut out the portrait and attach it with a brad or staple to the top of another sheet of drawing paper. **(20 points)**

_____ Lift the portrait and draw and write about the character's thoughts on the second page. (You can add extra sheets to show progression of thought.) **(20 points)**

_____ It should be neat and organized. **(15 points)**

_____ It should demonstrate effort and be colorful. **(15 points)**

_____ The student's name, the due date, and the period should be on the back. **(10 points)**

_____ **Total points earned**

HISTORICAL NEWSPAPER (100 POINTS)

_____ There are at least three articles written around the key events or ideas of the book. **(10 points)**

_____ Each article has a relevant title, and the newspaper is named. **(10 points)**

_____ Each article includes the who, what, when, where, why, and how. **(10 points)**

_____ There is one advertisement from the book's time period and one illustration to support one of the articles. **(10 points)**

_____ The articles should not have more than eight grammatical errors (spelling, sentence structure, word use, punctuation, etc.). **(10 points)**

_____ The articles should sound right, make sense, and look right. It should be neat and well organized. **(10 points)**

_____ The newspaper should represent the true format or layout of a newspaper. **(10 points)**

_____ The paper should be aged (using tea bags or some other method) to appear historical. **(10 points)**

_____ The articles should be on topic, interesting, and accurate. **(10 points)**

_____ The student's name, the due date, and the period should be present under the newspaper heading. **(10 points)**

_____ **Total points earned**

MOVIE POSTER (100 POINTS)

_____ The book title and author are present. **(10 points)**
_____ There are one or two sentences promoting the idea/theme of the book. **(20 points)**
_____ The illustration is big, bright, colorful, appealing, and well done. **(40 points)**
_____ The release date is included with the student's name and period. **(10 points)**
_____ The poster demonstrates effort and neatness. **(20 points)**
_____ **Total points earned**

SONG ABOUT THE BOOK (100 POINTS)

_____ The book title and author are present. **(10 points)**
_____ The student's name, the due date, and the period are present. **(10 points)**
_____ The song has a chorus that appears at least two times and depicts the problem or conflict. **(30 points)**
_____ The words chosen present the overall idea of the story. **(20 points)**
_____ The piece is typed or written neatly. **(20 points)**
_____ There are fewer than five grammatical errors (spelling, punctuation, etc.). **(10 points)**
_____ **Total points earned**

Professional References

Allen, J. (1999). *Words, Words, Words: Teaching Vocabulary in Grades 4–12.* Portland, ME: Stenhouse.

Allington, R. L. (2006). *What Really Matters for Struggling Readers: Designing Research-Based Programs.* 2nd ed. Boston: Pearson.

Auger, T. (2003). "Student-Centered Reading: A Review of the Research on Literature Circles." Retrieved June 30, 2008, from www.epsbooks.com/downloads/articles/Literature_Circles.pdf.

Beers, K. (2003). *When Kids Can't Read: What Teachers Can Do; A Guide for Teachers 6–12.* Portsmouth, NH: Heinemann.

Blachowicz, C., and P. J. Fisher. (2006). *Teaching Vocabulary in All Classrooms.* 3rd ed. Upper Saddle River, NJ: Pearson.

Brown, M. D. (2004). "Literature Circles Build Excitement for Books!" Retrieved January 28, 2009, from www.education-world.com/a_curr/curr259.shtml.

Daniels, H. (1994, 2002, 2004). Literature Circles: Voices and Choices in Book Clubs and Reading Groups. Portland, ME: Stenhouse.

Elliott, P. and D. Mays. (2001). *Literature Circles.* Retrived June 30, 2007, from www.edselect.com/DOCS/Litcir.pdf.

Gallagher, K. (2004). *Deeper Reading: Comprehension Challenging Texts, 4–12.* Portland, ME: Stenhouse.

Gilmore, D. P., and D. Day. (2006). "Let's Read, Write, and Talk about It: Literature Circles for English Learners." In *Supporting the Literacy Development of English Learners: Increasing Success in All Classrooms,* ed. T. A. Young and N. L. Hadaway, 194–209. Newark, DE: International Reading Association.

Gipe, J. P. (2006). *Multiple Paths to Literacy: Assessment and Differentiated Instruction for Diverse Learners, K–12.* 6th ed. Upper Saddle River, NJ: Pearson.

Haley, H. (1999). Public speech given at Seven Springs Middle School to the faculty, New Port Richey, FL.

Harvey, S. (1998). *Nonfiction Matters: Reading, Writing, and Research in Grades 3–8.* Portland, ME: Stenhouse.

Harvey, S., and A. Goudvis. (2000). *Strategies That Work: Teaching Comprehension to Enhance Understanding.* Markham, ON: Pembroke.

Hill, B. C., Johnson, N. J., and Schlick Noe, K. L. (1995, 2001, 2003). *Literature Circles and Response.* Norwood, MA: Christopher-Gordon.

Johnson, D. W., R. T. Johnson, and E. J. Holubec. (1994). *Cooperative Learning in the Classroom.* Alexandria, VA: ASCD.

Kagan, M. (2001). Logic line-ups: Higher-level thinking activities. San Clemente, CA: Kagan.

Kagan, S. (1992). *Cooperative Learning.* San Clemente, CA: Kagan.

Keene, E. O., and S. Zimmermann. (1997). *Mosaic of Thought: Teaching Comprehension in a Reader's Workshop.* Portsmouth, NH: Heinemann.

"Literature Circle." (n.d.). Retrieved June 28, 2008, from en.wikipedia.org/wiki/Literature_circle.

"Literature Circles." (2007). *ERIC Digest* 173. Retrieved January 28, 2009, from www.homeedsa.com/Articles/Literature%20Circles.asp.

McCormick, S. (2003). *Instructing Students Who Have Literacy Problems.* 4th ed. Upper Saddle River, NJ: Pearson.

Norton, D. E. (2005). *Multicultural Children's Literature: Through the Eyes of Many Children.* 2nd ed. Upper Saddle River, NJ: Pearson.

Pongratz, Susan G. (2005). *The Skilled Reader.* White Plains, NY: Pearson Longman.

Robb, Anina. (2003). *Fifty Reproducible Strategy Sheets That Build Comprehension during Independent Reading (Grades 4–8).* New York: Scholastic.

Robb, L. (2000). *Teaching Reading in Middle School: A Strategic Approach to Teaching Reading That Improves Comprehension and Thinking.* New York: Scholastic.

Roswell, Florence G., et al. (2005). *Diagnostic Assessment of Reading.* Rolling Meadows, IL: Riverside.

Schlick Noe, K. L. (2002). CD cover. Retrieved from http://www.litcircles.org/Extension/cd.html.

Schlick Noe, K. L. (2002). Character Bookmark. Retrieved from http://www.litcircles.org/Extenstion/cd.html.

Schlick Noe, K. L. (2002). Collage. Retrieved from http://www.litcircles.org/Extenstion/cd.html.

Schlick Noe, K. L. (2002). Game Board. Retrieved from http://www.litcircles.org/Extenstion/cd.html.

Schlick Noe, K. L. (2002). Map. Retrieved from http://www.litcircles.org/Extenstion/cd.html.

Schlick Noe, K. L. (2004). "Literature Circles Resource Center: Extension Projects." College of Education, Seattle University. Retrieved July 26, 2007, from www.litcircles.org/Extension/extension.html.

Sinatra, R. C., B. E. Blake, E. F. Guastello, and J. M. Robertson. (2007). *Reflective Literacy Practices in an Age of Standards: Engaging K–8 Learners.* Norwood, MA: Christopher-Gordon.

Thompson, Max. (2005). *Learning Focused Solutions*. Boone, NC: Learning-Focused.

Tompkins, G. E. (1998). *Fifty Literacy Strategies: Step by Step*. Upper Saddle River, NJ: Prentice-Hall.

Tovani, C. (2000). *I Read It, but I Don't Get It: Comprehension Strategies for Adolescent Readers*. Portland, ME: Stenhouse.

Tovani, C. (2004). *Do I Really Have to Teach Reading? Content Comprehension, Grades 6–12*. Portland, ME: Stenhouse.

Vacca, R. T., and J. L. Vacca. (2005). *Content Area Reading: Literacy and Learning across the Curriculum*. 8th ed. Boston: Pearson.

Woods, M. L., and A. J. Moe. (2003). *Analytical Reading Inventory: Comprehensive Assessment for All Students Including Gifted and Remedial*. 7th ed. Upper Saddle River, NJ: Pearson.

Literature References

Allen, Janet, and Patricia Daley. (2004). *Read-Aloud Anthology*. New York: Scholastic.

Anderson, Laurie Halse. (2000). *Fever 1793*. New York: Scholastic.

Binch, Caroline. (1994). *Gregory Cool*. New York: Dial Books for Young Readers.

Coerr, Eleanor. (1977). *Sadako and the Thousand Paper Cranes*. New York, NY: Putnam and Penguin Group.

Coville, Bruce. (1989). *My Teacher Is an Alien*. New York: Simon & Schuster.

Crane, Stephen. (1983). *The Red Badge of Courage*. New York, NY: Doherty.

Curtis, Christopher Paul. (1999). *Bud, Not Buddy*. New York, NY: Delacorte Press.

DeFelice, Cynthia. (2003). *Under the Same Sky*. New York: Farrar, Straus & Giroux.

Douglass, Frederick. (2004). *The Narrative Life of Frederick Douglass*. West Berlin, NJ: Townsend Press.

Draper, Sharon. (1994). *Tears of a Tiger*. New York: Simone Pulse.

Frank, Anne. (1995). *Anne Frank: The Diary of a Young Girl*, abridged and adapted by Mark Falstein. Belmont, CA: Fearon & Janus.

Greenfield, Eloise. (1988). *Grandpa's Face*. New York: Trumpet Club.

Guterson, David. (1995). *Snow Falling on Cedars* New York: Vintage Books.

Hawthorne, Nathaniel. (1959). *The Scarlet Letter*. New York: New American Library.

Hawthorne, Nathaniel. (2007). *The Scarlet Letter*. West Berlin, NJ: Townsend Press.

Lawson, Robert. (1988). *Ben and Me: An Astonishing Life of Benjamin Franklin by His Good Mouse Amos*. New York: Little.

Lowry, Lois. (1989). *Number the Stars*. New York: Laurel Leaf.

Matas, Carol. (1993). *Daniel's Story*. New York: Daniel Weiss Associates, Inc.

Petry, Ann. (1996). *Harriet Tubman*. New York, NY: HarperCollins.

Rose, Mary. (2002). *Week-by-Week Homework for Building Reading Comprehension and Fluency, Grades 3–6*. New York: Scholastic.

San Souci, Robert D. (1989). *The Talking Eggs*. New York: Scholastic.

Skerritt, Andrew. (2007). "Bringing Students the World." *St. Petersburg (Florida) Times*, November 6, *Pasco Times* 1.

Taylor, Mildred. (2002). *Roll of Thunder, Hear My Cry*. New York: Dial Press.

Wiesel, Elie. (2006). *Night*. New York: Hill & Wang.

Yolen, Jane. (1987). *Owl Moon*. New York: Scholastic.

About the Author

Lisa A. Fisher was a reading teacher and then a reading coach at a middle school in Pasco County, Florida. She now serves as a literacy coach at a high school. After graduating from the University of Southern Florida with a bachelor's degree in elementary education and a master's degree in reading education, Lisa has spent the majority of her teaching career at the secondary level, instructing a variety of students in reading.

Lisa has had several writing opportunities, and her passion for research and learning is clearly present in her written work. She has served as staff development coordinator, posting professional-development opportunities and plans for in-services that meet the school improvement plan. Lisa is also an adjunct instructor for Pasco-Hernando Community College, where she teaches remedial reading courses for college-bound adults.

Lisa now resides in Tampa, Florida. She enjoys life there with her husband and four beautiful Chihuahuas.

9 781607 094289

DATE DUE

HIGHSMITH